# Sure Steps to Reading and Spelling

### The Weiss Method of Teaching English

*By*
M. HERBERT WEISS
Ph.D., Th.D., H.L.D.

---

### REVISED EDITION

---

*Editor-in-Chief*
FLORENCE WEISS BLANK

*Co-Editor*
CAROLYN WEISS GUERTIN

---

WEISS PUBLISHING CO., INC.
5309 West Grace Street
Richmond, Virginia 23226
Telephone (804) 282-4641

COPYRIGHT © 1943, 1945, 1976 BY WEISS PUBLISHING CO., INC. ALL RIGHTS RESERVED

INTERNATIONAL STANDARD BOOK NUMBER 0-916720-02-0

*Notice!* The specialized application and plan of vowel and consonant sound recognition as developed and shown in the lessons of "Sure Steps to Reading and Spelling" and "The Science of Reading and Spelling" are original and must not be imitated in whole or in part. Patent applied for in the United States and foreign countries.

---

SURE STEPS TO READING AND SPELLING
Copyright 1945
By
The Weiss Publishing Company
Richmond, Virginia

SURE STEPS TO READING
Part One
Copyright 1943
By
M. Herbert Weiss, Th.D., H.L.D., Ph.D.

THE SCIENCE OF READING AND SPELLING
Copyright 1945
By
The Weiss Publishing Company
Richmond, Virginia

THE SCIENCE OF READING
Copyright 1943
By
M. Herbert Weiss, Th.D., H.L.D., Ph.D.

This book or parts thereof must not be reproduced in any form without written permission.

All rights reserved by The Weiss Publishing Company

Printed in the United States of America

To My Wife

Truly a Helpmeet

# FOREWORD

In this revision of *Sure Steps to Reading and Spelling,* the material has been left in the same sequence as it was in the previous editions in order to preserve the logical arrangement of the text and the unique features of this approach to teaching. The word lists and sentences in each lesson contain only those letters, sounds, and constructions that have been taught up to that point. Therefore, as soon as the new subject matter is presented, the student can decode all words in the lesson by himself. This is important for developing the learner's self-confidence and independence.

The same painstaking, scholarly research that characterized the previous editions of *Sure Steps* has been perpetuated in this revision. The new sections, additions, and explanations are designed to enhance the student's knowledge. They are the result of exhaustive investigation and analysis and are based upon actual teaching experience coupled with an awareness of the wide diversity in the learning processes of individuals. The Weiss Method incorporates successful techniques for motivating the pupil and for implementing his acquisition of skills in reading, comprehension, and spelling. In teaching *Sure Steps,* the instructor should not omit any lesson, since each one is a necessary stepping-stone and an integral part of the overall text.

Vowels are of prime importance in the structure of words. In the Weiss Method, the long vowels are taught initially for three significant reasons. First, with the exception of y (which uses the sound of i), the name of the letter is its long vowel sound, which is very easy for the pupil to remember. Second, many individuals experience difficulty with auditory differentiation and verbal reproduction of the short vowel sounds. Third, there is a simple, positive identification of the long vowel constructions. By observing the number of vowels and their position in the word, the student is able to determine whether the vowel is long or short.

The symbols used throughout the text (explained in the glossary facing Lesson 1) eliminate lengthy explanations and enable the non-reader to interpret at a glance the new constructions and rules. In most instances, illustrative words are supplied for visual reinforcement, providing the student with an opportunity to see the new construction in action. The advantage of the symbols is that the learner has flexibility in verbally expressing these rules, and he thereby avoids the memorized, conditioned response, in which he may repeat words mechanically, without understanding what he is saying.

Each lesson purposely contains some unfamiliar words which serve as a built-in test to evaluate the student's understanding of the new constructions.

Nonsense words are not used in the Weiss Method. Actual words are employed, although they may not be in the vocabulary of the reader or occasionally may be archaic. To read these words, the pupil must utilize the fundamentals taught, which strengthens his ability to decode independently.

When a person reads, the mind races ahead of the eyes to grasp the meaning of the phraseology. In other words, we frequently read by context, rather than by observing what actually is on the printed page. For example, in the sentence, "I have not eaten all day, so I am very . . . ," before the eyes actually see the word "hungry," the mind supplies it. In order to build accuracy and discourage guessing, the sentences in *Sure Steps* contain some disconnected subject matter, primarily in the early lessons. Likewise, a different word is sometimes substituted for an expected word in familiar expressions. If these facts are explained to the students, they will find the sentences challenging, motivating, and enjoyable.

Many inspirational and philosophical statements, interesting stories, and humorous anecdotes are scattered throughout the book. For instance, see the exercises in Lessons 84 and 85. Comprehension can be improved by encouraging the pupils to express in their own words the meaning of what they have read, especially in terms of their personal life experiences and goals. At the same time, the students can be motivated to increase their vocabulary by learning the definitions of the prefixes, suffixes, and word roots contained in the text. Other mind-sharpening techniques are group discussions of the subject matter and asking the learners questions that stimulate their thinking and do not merely elicit a stereotyped reply.

Because of the important and pertinent information it contains, the foreword to the 1946 edition has been reproduced in the current publication.

The voluminous notes left by our beloved parents, the late Dr. and Mrs. M. Herbert Weiss, have been an inspiration and of inestimable guidance in preparing this revision of *Sure Steps to Reading and Spelling*. In addition, we are deeply and sincerely indebted to a vast number of persons for their interest, comments, and suggestions, which have been so meaningful to us in this undertaking. We particularly express our gratitude to the late Harold H. Dervishian, Richmond City Council member and member of the Virginia House of Delegates, for his heartfelt interest, wisdom, and encouragement.

Florence Weiss Blank<br>Editor-in-Chief

January, 1976

# FROM THE
# FOREWORD TO THE 1946 EDITION

*Sure Steps to Reading and Spelling* is an entirely new method of teaching how to read and spell English quickly and easily according to sound. It was evolved during many years of actual classroom experience, and it has successfully overcome the reading and spelling difficulties of children of all ages, and native and foreign-born adults.

*Sure Steps* pupils learn to discern, to comprehend what they see, to listen carefully, and to be accurate. In many instances pupils have overcome stammering and other speech defects while learning the sounds of the letters by this method. Pupils who could not learn to read or to spell by any other method have learned by *Sure Steps to Reading and Spelling*.

The achievement of this method is that it supplants diacritical marks and the heavy load of word memory. *This method gives the pupil a definite guide to the relationship between the letters which form the word and the sound of the word.* He doesn't have to guess. He is taught to recognize constructions, and when he sees a word, to know by himself just what to do to read the word correctly without aid.

*Sure Steps to Reading and Spelling* teaches the value of the consonants and especially of the vowels in the composition of the word and how to recognize vowel constructions easily just from their position in the word. For instance, when the pupil masters a construction, he can read by himself every word in the English language that has that construction.

The book, *The Science of Reading and Spelling,* which explains in detail how to teach each lesson in *Sure Steps to Reading and Spelling,* will be of valuable assistance in teaching and understanding this method.

For their encouragement, we are greatly indebted to Dr. Dabney S. Lancaster, Virginia Superintendent of Education; Mr. W. C. Locker, Richmond Director of Writing and Adult Education; and Dr. Douglas S. Freeman, Editor of the *Richmond News Leader,* historian, and educator.

HENRIETTA WEISS
(Mrs. M. Herbert Weiss)

July, 1945

# TABLE OF CONTENTS

| Lesson | | Page |
|---|---|---|
| | Glossary of "Sign Language" | 10 |
| PART I—One-Syllable Words | | 11 |
| 1 | f, l, m, n, a, e, i | 11 |
| 2 | ai is a (long a) | 12 |
| 3 | ee is e, and ea is e (long e) | 13 |
| 4 | a_e is a, --ae is a, i_e is i, --ie is i, and --e is e (long vowels a, e, i) | 14 |
| 5 | h, r, s, and e_e is e (long e) | 15 |
| 6 | d, t | 16 |
| 7 | th--, --th, --the, _the, s, 's, s', --se | 18 |
| 8 | b, p | 20 |
| 9 | --ay is a (long a); --ay is ai | 21 |
| 10 | oa is o, o_e is o, --oe is o, --o is o (long o) | 23 |
| 11 | u_e is u, ui is u, --ue is u (long u) | 25 |
| 12 | --y is i, --ye is i, y_e is i (long y as long i) | 26 |
| Review Long Vowels | | 28 |
| 13 | a short | 29 |
| 14 | e short | 31 |
| 15 | i short, y short (short y as short i) | 32 |
| 16 | o short | 34 |
| 17 | u short | 36 |
| 18 | k | 38 |
| 19 | c (hard sound); c is k; ck is k | 39 |
| 20 | j | 42 |
| 21 | g (hard sound) | 43 |
| 22 | w | 45 |
| 23 | v; long and short vowels before v | 46 |
| 24 | y as a consonant | 48 |
| 25 | Two consonants at end of word, short and long a | 50 |
| 26 | Two consonants at end of word, short and long e | 52 |
| 27 | Two consonants at end of word, short i | 54 |
| 28 | Two consonants at end of word, short and long o | 55 |
| 29 | Two consonants at end of word, short u | 57 |
| 30 | sh | 59 |
| 31 | ch; tch | 61 |
| 32 | wh (read hw) | 63 |
| 33 | igh (-igh is i long, gh silent) | 64 |
| 34 | qu is kw | 65 |
| 35 | x is ks | 67 |
| 36 | z; alphabet | 69 |
| 37 | Two separately-sounded consonants at beginning of word, long a | 70 |
| 38 | Two separately-sounded consonants at beginning of word, short a; two separately-sounded consonants at beginning and two at end of word, short a | 71 |

| Lesson | | Page |
|---|---|---|
| 39 | Two separately-sounded consonants at beginning of word, long e | 73 |
| 40 | Two separately-sounded consonants at beginning of word, short e; two separately-sounded consonants at beginning and two at end of word, short e | 75 |
| 41 | Two separately-sounded consonants at beginning of word, long i; two separately-sounded consonants at beginning of word, short i; two separately-sounded consonants at beginning and two at end of word, short i | 76 |
| 42 | Two separately-sounded consonants at beginning of word, long o; two separately-sounded consonants at beginning of word, short o; two consonants at beginning and two at end of word, short o | 78 |
| 43 | Two separately-sounded consonants at beginning of word, long u and long y; two separately-sounded consonants at beginning of word, short u; two separately-sounded consonants at beginning and two at end of word, short u and short y | 80 |
| Review, short a-short e; long e-short i-short y; short o-short u; short e-short i-short y | | 83 |
| PART II—Words of more than one syllable, suffixes and prefixes | | 85 |
| Introduction to Lesson 44; y at end of word | | 85 |
| 44 | Two-syllable words, suffixes -ly, -ful, -less, -ness | 86 |
| 45 | Two-syllable words, suffix -y; two-syllable words ending in --ie; two-syllable words ending in --ey | 88 |
| 46 | Two-syllable words, suffix -ing; adding suffix -ing to words ending in -ie | 91 |
| 47 | Two-syllable words, suffix -ed (meaning past time), e silent; suffix -ed, e silent, d with sound of t, after x, f, s, sh, ch, p, k, ck | 93 |
| 48 | Suffix -ed, e sounded after d and t | 96 |
| 49 | Suffixes -s and -es; -es forms syllable after hissing sounds: s, sh, x, z, ch | 98 |
| 50 | Suffix -er, meaning "more," comparative degree adjectives or adverbs; suffix -er, meaning person who or thing which does whatever root word indicates (nouns); and -er not suffixed | 100 |
| 51 | Suffix -est, meaning "most," superlative degree adjectives or adverbs; and -ish, meaning like, belonging to, or of nature of | 103 |
| 52 | Two-syllable words; prefix a-; |

# TABLE OF CONTENTS—(Continued)

| Lesson | | Page |
|---|---|---|
| | "ick" rule; spelling of "k" sound is determined in each syllable individually | 105 |
| 53 | Two-syllable words, prefixes ex-, un-, re-, de- | 109 |
| 54 | u as in "pull"; vowel before v: long; short; both long and short, as in "live" | 111 |
| 55 | Three consonants at beginning of word, scr-, spl-, spr-, str-, squ-; three consonants at end of word | 113 |
| 56 | al (as in "all") | 115 |
| 57 | air, -are (long a before r) | 117 |
| 58 | ar sounded as r (short a before r); five sounds of A | 119 |
| 59 | arr, ara, are, ari, aro, aru, ary (before end of root word) (sound of "a" in "ask" or "at" and schwa sound) | 121 |
| 60 | wa, war, qua, quar, wha, whar (sound of "a" as in "all" and as short "o") | 123 |
| | Review long and short vowels | 125 |
| | Drill—long and short vowels | 127 |
| 61 | or, oar, ore | 128 |
| 62 | "er" sound, spelled er, ir, ur, yr, our, ear followed by consonant; -or and -ar slurred like er | 130 |
| 63 | wor sounded as wer | 133 |
| 64 | Seven sounds of ea | 134 |
| 65 | o and ou like u in "rude" or in "put" | 137 |
| 66 | Prefixes fore- and for- | 138 |
| 67 | Prefixes per-, pre-, pro- | 139 |
| 68 | Ending -le in two-syllable words; -le in three-or-more-syllable words; suffixing -le words | 141 |
| 69 | -ind, -ild (long i sound) | 144 |
| 70 | -old, -olt, -ost, -oll (long o sound); more-than-one-syllable root words ending in -ol having long o sound | 146 |
| 71 | Three-syllable words; double suffixes | 148 |
| 72 | Soft c (like s); ce; after soft c, e is sounded in -es | 149 |
| 73 | Soft c (like s); ci, cy | 151 |
| 74 | ci as sh (followed by vowel and not in first syllable of root word); -cial, -cian, -cient, -ciency, -ciate, -cious; -ci as shee; -ce as sh; -ous ending indicates adjective; -us ending indicates noun; -an ending indicates person, adjective, or geographical location | 154 |
| 75 | ti as sh (followed by vowel and not in first syllable of root word); -tion, -tian, -tient, -tiate, -tial, -tious; after s, sound ti as ch | 156 |
| 76 | si as sh or zh (followed by vowel and not in first syllable of root word); after consonant, sound si as sh, -ssion and -sion; after vowel, sound si as zh, -sion; after r, sound -sion as zhun, shun; xi as k-sh, -xion, -xious; su as shu and zhu; after vowel, su as zhu | 158 |
| 77 | Soft g (like j); ge; after soft g, e sounded in -es; words ending in ge followed by single consonant which is part of root word; ange as ainge; more-than-one-syllable words ending in ge, vowel before ge either long or short; soft g as zh; retaining e after soft g when next letter is not i or y | 161 |
| 78 | Soft g (like j); gi, gy; hard and soft c; gg has hard sound; root words with hard g followed by e, i, or y; suffixed words, hard g remains hard even when followed by e, i, or y | 163 |
| 79 | tu as chu (not in first syllable of root word, long u construction) | 166 |
| 80 | ei as long a; eigh as long a (ei as long a, gh silent); ey as long a | 167 |
| 81 | ei and ie as ee (long e); ei after c; ie after other consonants; ei or ie after s | 168 |
| 82 | y preceded by consonant changed to i when suffix is added; one-syllable root words, change y to i, generally, only when adding -ed, -er, -es, and -est; y not changed to i when vowel precedes y; y not changed to i when adding suffix beginning with i | 170 |
| 83 | Verbs ending in --fy and --ly (y long); long y changed to long i when suffix is added; long y changed to short i when suffix is added (mainly -cation) | 172 |
| | PART III—Compound vowels and consonants; two vowels side by side, both sounded; two consonants side by side, one silent; homonyms | 174 |
| 84 | Long oo (as in food) | 174 |
| 85 | Short oo (as in book) | 176 |
| 86 | au, aw | 178 |
| 87 | ough as au (gh silent); four words beginning with th and containing ough (different sounds of ough) | 179 |
| 88 | ou (as in our), ow, ough | 181 |
| 89 | ou (long o as in soul), ow, ough; nine sounds of ou | 183 |
| 90 | oi, oy | 186 |
| 91 | eu, ew (long u sounds) | 188 |
| 92 | Two vowels side by side, both sounded; long vowel digraph, only first vowel sounded; long vowel digraph backwards, both vowels | |

# TABLE OF CONTENTS—(Continued)

| Lesson | | Page |
|---|---|---|
| | sounded; compound vowels and diphthongs backwards, both vowels sounded; long vowel digraph at end of root word, only first vowel sounded; when not at end of root word, both vowels sounded; --iac (short a, but k dropped from ck digraph); examples of diphthong, compound, or long vowel combinations in which both vowels are sounded | 190 |
| | Review long vowels and compound vowels | 196 |
| 93 | gh as f | 197 |
| 94 | ph as f | 198 |
| 95 | ch as k; ch silent; ch as sh | 200 |
| 96 | gn in same syllable, g silent; words beginning or ending with gn, g silent; words ending in gn, g remains silent generally when adding suffixes -s, -er, -or, -ee, -ing, -ed, -ment; gn not in same syllable, sound both; gm in same syllable, g silent; gm not in same syllable, sound both | 202 |
| 97 | wr (w silent) | 205 |
| 98 | kn (k silent) | 206 |

| Lesson | | Page |
|---|---|---|
| 99 | -lk, -lm, -lf, -lve, -ld (l silent); when not in same syllable, sound both | 208 |
| 100 | -mb, -bt (b silent); when not in same syllable, sound both; -sten, -ften, -stle (t silent) | 210 |
| 101 | h silent; gh, rh (h silent); ps, pn, pt (p silent) | 212 |
| 102 | mn (n silent); when not in same syllable, sound both | 214 |
| 103 | que at end of word (q as k and ue silent); qu as k; que and quet as "kay"; gue at end of word (g hard, ue silent); gu as gw; gu as hard g; u as w; o as w; oi as wah; oua as wa | 216 |
| | "The Tongue" | 219 |
| | Quotation: "If thou lackest knowledge" | 220 |
| | Homonyms | 221 |
| | Consonant Sounds (chart) | 228 |
| | Index (including list of abbreviations, anecdotes, contractions, exceptions, exceptions (special categories), jokes, non-phonics, reviews, riddles, and stories) | 229 |

# GLOSSARY OF "SIGN LANGUAGE"
(Explanation of symbols to enable the non-reader to be independent in interpreting constructions and rules)

| EXAMPLE | MEANS |
|---|---|
| ai = a | AI says (or spells) A. Example: tr**ai**n. (Special vowel digraph = long vowel sound). (Two special vowels side by side = long vowel sound). |
| e_e = e | E one consonant E says (or spells) E. Example: th**e**m**e**. The symbol _ denotes a space in which a consonant is to be inserted between the two vowels. (Vowel-one consonant-vowel = long vowel sound). |
| - - ue = u | UE at the end of the word says (or spells) U. Examples: h**ue**, contin**ue**. In this construction, the symbol - - means "at the end of the word." It does **not** represent the number of letters in the word nor whether they are vowels or consonants, nor does it represent the number of syllables in the word. |
| th - - | TH at the beginning of the word. In this construction, the symbol - - means "at the beginning of the word." It does **not** represent the number of letters in the word nor whether they are vowels or consonants, nor does it represent the number of syllables in the word. In the example shown, TH at the beginning of the word has the voiceless sound in **th**esis or the voiced sound in **th**ese. |
| road − ro̸ad = rod | ROAD, take out A, says (or spells) ROD. |
| rode − rod̸e = rod | RODE, take out E, says (or spells) ROD. |
| igh = i | IGH says (or spells) I. Example: h**igh**. |
| —ly | Suffix. Example: year**ly**. In this construction, the symbol — means "attached to the end of the word." In this particular illustration, letters in the word precede LY. |
| dis— | Prefix. Example: **dis**connect. In this construction, the symbol — means "attached to the beginning of the word." In this particular illustration, letters in the word follow DIS. |

# PART I

## ONE-SYLLABLE WORDS

---

### LESSON 1

1.     F         L         M         N

2.     f         l         m         n

3.     F f       L l       M m       N n

4.     A         E         I

5.     a         e         i

6.     A a       E e       I i

7.     L l       I i       **I l**

8.   Ai     Ea     Ee     ai     ea     ee

# LESSON 2

**ai = a**
**ai**m

| 1 | 2 |
|---|---|
| aim | maim |
| ail | mail |
| fai_ | fail |
| lai_ | lain |
| mai_ | main |
| nai_ | nail |
| fai_ | fain |

## DRILL

| | | |
|---|---|---|
| Mail | Nail | Main |
| Maim | Aim | Fail |
| Lain | Ail | Fain |

## EXERCISES

1. I aim. I ail.
2. I mail a nail. A main nail.
3. Aim a nail. A main aim.

# LESSON 3

| ee = e | ea = e |
|:---:|:---:|
| **ee**l | l**ea**f |

| 1 | 2 | 3 | 4 |
|---|---|---|---|
| eel | fee | meal | mean |
| Lee | feel | lean | leaf |

## DRILL

| | | | | |
|---|---|---|---|---|
| ail | eel | mail | meal | aim |
| fail | feel | Lee | leaf | lain |
| lean | main | mean | Lea | maim |
| fain | fee | nail | Neal | leal |

## EXERCISES

1. I feel a nail. I feel a leaf.
2. A lean meal. A lean eel.
3. A main meal. I lean.
4. Lee, mail Neal a fee.

13

# LESSON 4

| a_e = a | - - ae = a | i_e = i | - - ie = i | - - e = e |
|---------|------------|---------|------------|-----------|
| name    | Fae        | fine    | lie        | me        |

| 1 | 2 |
|---|---|
| male | file |
| lame | life |
| mane | mile |
| fame | nine |
| Mame | lime |
| lane | mine |

*Contraction:* I'll

| lie  | Fae | mime | ale  | I'll | Mame |
|------|-----|------|------|------|------|
| fife | fie | Mae  | Nile | line | me   |

## EXERCISES

1. A nail file. A fine nail. A fine fife.
2. A fine line. A nine mile line. A lie.
3. A fine nail file. A lean meal. A fine ale.
4. I feel fine. A fine life. A life line.
5. Mail Mame a nail file.
6. Lee, mail me a fine nail file.
7. "Mae - I mean Fae, name a mine."
8. I'll name a mine, "Lea Mine." I'll file a nail.
9. A nine mile lane. A main line.
10. A lame male. I'll fine Lee.
11. I'll name a lane, "Fae Lane."

## LESSON 5

| H h | S s | R r | e_e = e here |
|---|---|---|---|

| 1 | 2 | 3 | 4 | 5 |
|---|---|---|---|---|
| hail | hear | hale | here | hire |
| sail | seal | safe | sere | sire |
| rain | reel | same | mere | rife |

## DRILL

| he | fear | rise | rear | mire |
|---|---|---|---|---|
| ear | here | seen | fire | real |
| ire | ream | near | rile | hie |
| rail | sane | reef | raise | lease |

*Contraction:*  *he'll*

| 1 | | | 2 | | |
|---|---|---|---|---|---|
| sail | - | sale | see | - | sea |
| hail | - | hale | seem | - | seam |
| hear | - | here | leer | - | Lear |

| 3 | | | | | |
|---|---|---|---|---|---|
| seer | - | sere | - | sear | |
| heel | - | heal | - | he'll | |

## LESSON 5—(Continued)

## EXERCISES

1. I see Mae. Fae sees me. Rae sees Lee.
2. I hear, "Fire!" I see a fire near here. I hear Fae.
3. I fear fire. I feel safe near Neal. I'll rise.
4. Lea, I feel safe here. I see mire. I lie here.
5. I see a real fire sale near here. I hear a lie.
6. Lease means hire. I'll hire Mame. He'll hire Fae.
7. I'll raise a real seal. Lee sees a seal.
8. Neal, hire Rae. I hear Mae. Mae here? He'll hire me.
9. I'll lease a reel. He sees a reef. I see a fife.
10. I see hail. I hear rain. I see a safe.

## LESSON 6

### D d

### T t

| aid | feed | tie | date | dame |
|---|---|---|---|---|
| ate | feet | die | hate | Dane |
| fade | need | side | meat | dean |
| fate | neat | site | tail | dine |
| laid | seed | tire | meet | read |
| late | seat | dire | tease | ride |
| maid | heed | tide | deed | mite |
| mate | heat | rite | made | feat |
| raid | deem | tile | deer | tea |
| rate | team | hide | deal | eat |
| dale | dear | dime | lead | teen |
| tale | tear | time | tame | teem |

## LESSON 6—(Continued)

| 1 | | | 2 | | |
|---|---|---|---|---|---|
| maid | - | made | feet | - | feat |
| tail | - | tale | read | - | reed |
| team | - | teem | aid | - | aide |
| dear | - | deer | tee | - | tea |
| he'd | - | heed | | | |

| | | 3 | | |
|---|---|---|---|---|
| tees | - | teas | - | tease |
| meat | - | meet | - | mete |

## EXERCISES

1. I deal here. I need meat. I hide a dime.
2. I hate meat. I'll eat lean meat.
3. I feed a deer. I dine here. I mean I eat here.
4. I read a line. I need a seat. I'll eat late.
5. He ate late. Rae made tea. I see a lime seed.
6. I'll read. I need time. I'll read a tale.
7. I ride a mile. I see I need a tire.
8. Heed me. Aid a team mate.
9. I see a neat maid. I made a date. I'll meet Fae here.
10. Lee sees me. I see Lee. He'll meet me here.
11. I hide. I tease Dale. I heed Neal.
12. I see a tame deer. I see a deer hide.
13. Dear Mae, I'll die. I need aid. Aid me.
14. I laid tile. I need heat. Nate made a fire.
15. I'll ride. I need a dime. I meet a dean.
16. I need a tie. I see a fine tie.
17. I need a maid. I'll hire a maid. He'll hire a maid.
18. He'll lead Nate here. I see a reed. I need a lease.

# LESSON 7

|  th - -  | - - th | - - the | _the |
|---|---|---|---|
| **th**eme | tee**th** | tee**the** | la**the** |
| **th**ese | | | |

| s | 's | s' | - - se |
|---|---|---|---|
| eel**s** | maid**'s** | maid**s'** | lea**se** |
| dine**s** | | | |

| th | s | s | 's   s' | - - se |
|---|---|---|---|---|
| the | maids | hears | Dale's | raise |
| Thee | heels | eats | Lee's | lease |
| these | seats | leads | Rae's | tease |
| theme | meats | heats | deer's | |
| Thine | ties | meets | Fae's | |
| faith | dimes | dies | Neal's | |
| teeth | limes | aids | maid's | |
| teethe | miles | needs | maids' | |
| seethe | deeds | dines | team's | |
| lathe | meals | reads | teams' | |
| tithe | names | hides | dean's | |
| lithe | teams | rides | seal's | |

*Non-Phonic:* are

## LESSON 7—(Continued)

## EXERCISES

1. The maids eat here. These are the maids' seats.
2. These are the teams' aims. The teams meet here.
3. Rae eats lean meat. These are Lee's nails.
4. These are real teeth. Mae hears the maid.
5. These are the deer's feet. These are the deer's teeth.
6. The maids eat meat. Mame eats a lime.
7. The aide meets me here. Rae reads Lea's theme.
8. These are the maids' meals. The maids ate here nine times. Fae needs teeth.
9. Mae reads nine tales. These are the same tales I read.
10. Lee reads Dale's theme. I read the mail.
11. Nate rides nine miles. He needs time.
12. Are these the aide's files? These files are mine.
13. Rae hears me read these lines. Rae's maid needs aid.
14. I tithe a dime. Lee needs faith. I tease Nate.
15. Are these Neal's nails? Fae's deeds are fine.
16. "Are these seals tame?" "The tame seals are Lee's."
17. He dines near here. Are the meals dear here?
18. He heats the meat. He eats the deer meat.
19. Are these rails safe? The maids are safe near the rails.
20. Nate reads the maid's mail. He heeds me.
21. Are these deer's hides? Neal needs a lathe.
22. Are these Lee's tires? Lee's tires are near the side rails.
23. The dean reads the theme. Rae made Lea seethe.
24. He needs a lease. I need a raise.

# LESSON 8

**B b**　　　**P p**

| b p | b d p | b p d | d b p | d p b | p b d | p d b | d t |
|---|---|---|---|---|---|---|---|
| Abe | ape | beam | | | peas | | beef |
| base | tape | babe | | | pile | | heap |
| bathe | paid | bean | | | pate | | leap |
| bait | nape | bite | | | pies | | reap |
| bane | seep | bead | | | peep | | peer |
| beer | pie | bide | | | deep | | ripe |
| beep | neap | pipe | | | bile | | pine |

**1**

bail - bale
pail - pale
Pete - peat

**2**

pain - pane
beat - beet
peel - peal

**3**

be - bee - Bea

*Non-Phonic:* been

## EXERCISES

1. Pete eats beef. Abe eats beets.
2. He peels the beets. These are Bea's beads.
3. Pete beats the ape. The ape leaps.
4. The ape bites Pete. Pete feels pain.
5. "Are these apes tame?" "Dean's apes are tame."

## LESSON 8—(Continued)

6. "Are these Abe's pails?" "The pails are mine."
7. These pails are deep. Pile the deep pails here.
8. The pale maid made a pie. Pete eats the pie.
9. Abe eats beans. Bea eats peas. I bite the pie.
10. Pete hides Abe's pipe. Abe peeps.
11. He sees Pete hide the pipe. I paid Abe a dime.
12. "Are these peas dear?" "The beets are dear."
13. I'll dine here. I'll be here late. Neal ate beef.
14. I feel a pain. I'll bathe late.
15. "Are these dates ripe?" "These are ripe dates."
16. Pete eats the dates. Abe eats the ripe dates.
17. Pile the pails here. Tape the tales.

## LESSON 9

- - ay = a
say

- - ay = ai-

| may | lay | ray |
| say | hay | day |
| bay | pay | nay |
| days | rays | pays |
| May's | Fay's | lays |

*Non-Phonic:* *they* *hey* *says* *said*

## LESSON 9—(Continued)

### EXERCISES

1. They say they lay rails near the bay.
2. Bea says they'll lay a nine mile rail here.
3. They say May days are fine days.
4. These are May days. Fay lay near the bay.
5. May I bathe here? May I dine near the bay?
6. Fay feels the rays. Fay feels the heat.
7. Ray says these are fine May days.
8. Fay feeds the deer hay. The deer eats hay.
9. "Hey, Pete, may I lay the hay here?" "Pile the hay here."
10. He says, "Pay a dime a day." I say, "I paid Fay."
11. "May I see the beads?" "Here they are, see?"
12. "Are these real beads?" "Abe said they are."
13. I said, "Pay the maid." They said they paid the maid.
14. Fay said, "I'll be paid." "Hey, Fay, see the rays!"
15. I see the rays. Rays are beams. Beams are rays.
16. Pete said he'll pay me a dime a day.

## LESSON 10

O o

| oa = o | o_e = o | - - oe = o | - - o = o |
|--------|---------|------------|-----------|
| r**oa**d | r**o**d**e** | t**oe** | n**o** |

| soap | note | doe | so | oat | hole |
|------|------|-----|-----|------|------|
| foam | tone | roe | no | lobe | bone |
| moan | sole | toe | lo | loaf | pole |
| boat | home | foe | rose | tote | dole |
| loam | robe | Poe | role | oath | rope |
| toad | nose | mope | those | dome | mode |
| loath | pope | dose | hope | foal | mole |
| loathe | hose | tome | pose | Nome | hone |

|  1  |  |  |  2  |  |  |
|-----|---|---|-----|---|---|
| road | - | rode | mote | - | moat |
| lone | - | loan | load | - | lode |
| roam | - | Rome | hoe | - | ho |

*Non-Phonic:* one  to  do  don't
*Exception:* too

### EXERCISES

1. One day Rose rode to Rome to see the pope.
2. Nate says he, too, hopes to see the pope.
3. Do these roads lead to Rome?
4. No, these roads don't lead to Rome. They lead to the mines.
5. One lone road leads to Sea-Side Lane.

## LESSON 10—(Continued)

6. Pete roams the road. He totes the loam.
7. I see the sea foam. He sees the dome.
8. I see nine life boats. They load the boats.
9. "They tie the boats." "No, they don't tie boats."
10. "They do so tie the sail boats to those poles."
11. Don't loaf. Don't moan. Don't mope.
12. Read the note. The note says, "Rose needs hose."
13. Fay, too, needs hose. May's toe-nails made those holes. Fay needs a robe, too.
14. "Do these hose fade?" "No, fine hose don't fade."
15. Abe bathes. He needs soap. He needs the robe.
16. "They say the foe roams these roads."
17. "No, don't fear; they don't roam here."
18. I hear Rose made oat-meal to-day. I don't eat oat-meal.
19. I do eat meat loaf. I do eat roe.
20. These are the home-made pies Rose made to-day.
21. I rode nine miles to-day. I'll be home late.
22. I hope to be home to-day. Don't be too late!

# LESSON 11

## U u

| u_e = u | ui = u | - - ue = u |
|---------|--------|------------|
| **mule** | **suit** | **due** |

| use | suit | sue | rule | tune |
| fume | Muir | due | ruse | dune |
| lure | pure | hue | nude | lute |
| fuse | rude | rue | muse | Rube |
| mute | tube | mule | dupe | dude |

*Exception:* *suite*

*Abbreviations:* *a.m.  A.M.  p.m.  P.M.*

## EXERCISES

1. I need a mule. I'll hire a mule.
2. I'll hire a tame mule. I'll ride the mule.
3. Rube, tie the mule to the rail. Feed the mule.
4. Rube feeds the mule pure oats.
5. The mule eats oats. A mule eats hay, too.
6. Pete rides a mule. He beats the mule.
7. I say to Pete, "Don't be rude to the mule."
8. I hope he'll rue the day he beat the mule.
9. Mules are mute. They don't say they feel pain.
10. Don't be rude to the mute. Don't be mean.
11. Sue made a rule to be home nine p.m.
12. Due to the rain, I'll be late to-day.
13. Rose says, "I'll sue Rube Muir." I say, "Don't sue Rube."

## LESSON 11—(Continued)

14. These are the rules Sue says to heed.
15. Don't be rude. Use no ruse. Don't lure.
16. "Sue's hose are rose hue. They don't fade."
17. "Don't dupe Sue. They do so fade."
18. Sue needs the fuse. I don't see the fuse.
19. I use pure soap. I feed the mule pure oats.
20. Sue, use the hoe. I need the hoe, too.
21. These tubes are mine. Don't use those tubes here.
22. Neal needs the rope. I'll use the rope to tie the mule to the pole.
23. One p.m., Sue rides the mule near the dune. The dude rides the mule, too.

## LESSON 12

Y y

y = i

- - y = i
my

- - ye = i
rye

y_e = i
type

| by | thy | dye | lye | lyre | dyne |
| bye | my | rye | type | pyre | Lyle |

*Non-Phonic:* eye   eyes   buy   hi   thyme
*Vowels or Helpers:* a   e   i   o   u   y

## LESSON 12—(Continued)

## EXERCISES

1. I buy my meat here. I buy oats here, too.
2. Rose buys a rye loaf. Fay eats rye.
3. I'll buy pure rye. They eat pure rye.
4. I'll dye my hose. I'll buy the dye here.
5. Sue says, "I need lye. I use lye." May says, "O, Sue, don't lie."
6. Sue says, "I say I use lye. I don't mean I lie."
7. "I don't mean I'll die. I mean I'll buy dye."
8. A pyre means a fire. I see a lyre.
9. Rose types a note. I read the note.
10. Dale types nine lines by the time I type one line.
11. These tales are by Hy Lyle.
12. These are my eyes. Those are Rae's eyes.
13. I use my eyes to read. My eyes lead me.
14. My eyes see the road. The eyes see. The eye sees.
15. I type my notes. I type Mae's notes.
16. I'll type Dean's notes, too.
17. I'll buy beets. I'll buy peas. He'll buy beef.
18. Hi, Rose! Bye, Nate! Bye, bye!

# REVIEW

## Long Vowels

| | | | | | |
|---|---|---|---|---|---|
| ai = a | - | ail | aim | maid | paid |
| - - ae = a | - | Mae | Rae | Fae | |
| a_e = a | - | ate | ale | late | same |
| - - ay = a | - | day | say | lays | rays |
| ea = e | - | eat | ear | sea | meat |
| ee = e | - | eel | see | feel | meet |
| e_e = e | - | here | mere | sere | |
| - - e = e | - | he | me | be | |
| - - ie = i | - | lie | die | ties | pies |
| i_e = i | - | dime | mile | fine | tide |
| oa = o | - | oat | oath | road | loaf |
| - - oe = o | - | hoe | toe | roe | foe |
| o_e = o | - | rode | nose | home | hope |
| - - o = o | - | no | so | lo | ho |
| ui = u | - | suit | | | |
| - - ue = u | - | due | sue | hue | rue |
| u_e = u | - | use | fuse | mule | tube |
| - - ye = i | - | dye | rye | lye | bye |
| y_e = i | - | type | pyre | lyre | dyne |
| - - y = i | - | by | my | thy | |

| a | e | i | o | u | y |
|---|---|---|---|---|---|
| ai | ea | | oa | ui | |
| - - ae | ee | - - ie | - - oe | - - ue | - - ye |
| a_e | e_e | i_e | o_e | u_e | y_e |
| - - ay | - - e | | - - o | | - - y |

# LESSON 13

> Short A                    at

### 1

| | | | | |
|---|---|---|---|---|
| aim | - | a̸im | = | am |
| aid | - | a̸id | = | ad |
| main | - | ma̸in | = | man |
| rain | - | ra̸in | = | ran |
| maid | - | ma̸id | = | mad |
| paid | - | pa̸id | = | pad |
| pain | - | pa̸in | = | pan |
| laid | - | la̸id | = | lad |
| bait | - | ba̸it | = | bat |

### 2

| | | | | |
|---|---|---|---|---|
| ate | - | at̸e | = | at |
| fate | - | fat̸e | = | fat |
| hate | - | hat̸e | = | hat |
| rate | - | rat̸e | = | rat |
| tape | - | tap̸e | = | tap |
| pane | - | pan̸e | = | pan |
| made | - | mad̸e | = | mad |
| nape | - | nap̸e | = | nap |
| bathe | - | bath̸e | = | bath |

## DRILL

| at | am | as | an | ham |
|---|---|---|---|---|
| tan | has | tab | Sam | Dan |
| sad | hat | ram | ran | add |
| sat | fan | than | map | lap |
| mat | had | man | fat | pan |
| dad | mass | that | bad | lab |
| pass | bath | pat | pad | bat |
| rap | path | lad | nap | bass |
| ban | nab | sap | hath | fad |

## LESSON 13—(Continued)

### EXERCISES

1. I ate at home. I had some ham.
2. Sam ate at Dan's. He had some pie.
3. Ann has a tan hat. Dan has no hat.
4. Ann's dad has a tam.
5. I am mad at that fat man.
6. He said that I am rude. Rude means bad.
7. That fat man ran to see my dad.
8. I hear a rap. I ran to meet the man.
9. I need a road map. I need a pad.
10. Dad hears me read. He sees me add.
11. Pam sat near my dad. Dad said, "Read the tale to Pam."
12. I read day by day. Day by day I add.
13. Ann said, "I may pass." I said, "I hope so."
14. My dad made me a bat. Dan sees my bat. One day he said, "May I use the bat?"
15. I hire a man. The man made the path that leads to my home.
16. I pay the man by the day. He needs aid. He has no teeth. He ails.
17. Nan said, "That made me feel sad."
18. I made tea, so he had tea and pie.
19. He had a dime, so he rode home that day.
20. One day I said to Tad, "I need a pad."
21. He said he had no pad. I need a dime to buy a pad.
22. Sam and Dan are at Ann's. They ate at Ann's to-day at one p.m.
23. They had ham and beans, pie and tea.
24. Dan sat near me, and Ann's dad sat by my side. They had no hats.
25. Sam and Dan are pals. They are fine lads.
26. Sam has a boat. The boat has a sail. Sam sails the boat at the bay.
27. I see a man pass by. I say "Hi!" to the man.
28. The man says "Hi!" to me. He said he feels bad, so I ran to aid the man.
29. I had no one to aid me. I said, "May-be I'll lead the man home."

# LESSON 14

**Short E**

net
**Ed**

| 1 | | | | 2 | | | |
|---|---|---|---|---|---|---|---|
| neat | - | ne̸at | = | net | feel | - | fe̸el | = | fell |
| mean | - | me̸an | = | men | feed | - | fe̸ed | = | fed |
| lead | - | le̸ad | = | led | meet | - | me̸et | = | met |
| read | - | re̸ad | = | red | beet | - | be̸et | = | bet |
| seal | - | se̸al | = | sell | peep | - | pe̸ep | = | pep |
| dean | - | de̸an | = | den | Pete | - | Pet̸e | = | pet |

## DRILL

| let | hen | bed | pet | ten |
| Ben | set | pen | bell | less |
| ebb | dell | hem | Nell | Beth |
| then | them | tell | mess | Bess |

*Non-Phonic:* there their theirs
*Contractions:* there's they're

## EXERCISES

1. I hear a bell. One bell means time to eat.
2. Nine bells means "to bed."
3. I see ten hens. I feed the hens.
4. I made a rule to feed the hens at ten a.m.
5. I feed the mules. Then I eat.
6. I fed them pure oats to-day.
7. I'll tell Ben to sell the red hens.

## LESSON 14—(Continued)

8. Mel tells me he met ten men at sea.
9. They had a net there. They had red hats.
10. Ted has a pen. He lets me use the pen.
11. Pete has a fine pen. Ned has no pen.
12. Dan has a red pen. Bess needs a pen.
13. I see one man here. Sam sees nine men there.
14. Ed sees ten men. I don't see them.
15. I am dad's pet. I feed my pet at nine a.m.
16. At nine a.m. I read. At ten a.m. I eat.
17. At one p.m. I fed my hens and my mules.
18. The hen eats seeds. Hens eat less than mules.
19. There are my pets. As a rule they are fed at ten.
20. Ann eats less than Beth. I eat less than they do.
21. Those men don't see. I led them to their beds.
22. Here are their hats. There are their robes.
23. My eyes see. My ears hear.

## LESSON 15

Short I        it

| 1 | | | | 2 | | | |
|---|---|---|---|---|---|---|---|
| hide | - | hid*e* | = | hid | dime | - | dim*e* | = | dim |
| ripe | - | rip*e* | = | rip | ride | - | rid*e* | = | rid |
| pine | - | pin*e* | = | pin | bite | - | bit*e* | = | bit |
| file | - | fil*e* | = | fill | mile | - | mil*e* | = | mill |
| tile | - | til*e* | = | till | pile | - | pil*e* | = | pill |

## LESSON 15—(Continued)

## DRILL

| if   | it   | is   | in   | Bill |
|------|------|------|------|------|
| sit  | his  | fin  | inn  | hit  |
| hiss | sin  | hill | mill | this |
| tin  | thin | miss | pit  | ill  |
| till | bit  | lip  | fit  | pill |
| lid  | rim  | pin  | bin  | rib  |
| rid  | rip  | sip  | mid  | hid  |
| hip  | dim  | did  | him  | tip  |
| sill | Bim  | bib  | dip  | nip  |
| tiff | din  | dill | bid  | rill |

**Short Y = Short I**          myth

myth          Lynn          Syd

## EXERCISES

1. Bill feels ill to-day. He is in bed in the den.
2. So I sit near his bed. I read to him.
3. I sat there till mid-day. Then Miss Ann Pyle made tea. Miss Pyle tells Bill to sip the tea.
4. Lynn reads the myth to Syd.
5. Bim hits his mule in the ribs.
6. Bim's dad tells him that it is a sin to hit the mule.
7. Bim is mean. He said he'll hit me, too. I said I'll tell his dad.
8. That hat fits me. This hat fits Syd.
9. That man sells hats. This man sells fine pins.
10. I don't see the bill. There is the bill.
11. I'll pay that bill to-day.
12. I don't see Bill. There is Bill. He hid in the bin.

## LESSON 15—(Continued)

13. My hat has a rim. Don't rip it. That hat has no rim.
14. This is a tin pan. This pan has a hole in its side.
15. That is a thin tin pan. Here is one that has a lid to fit it.
16. This pan is too thin, and that tin pan is too dear.
17. I'll buy this one. It suits me.
18. My name is Mel. My dad's name is Nate.
19. This man's name is Sam. That man's name is Ben.
20. Lil needs a pin. Mae needs ten pins. There are the pins.
21. Beth has red lips. Ray has red lips, too.
22. Dear Nell, tell Hy to see me late to-day.
23. Don't miss. Tell him this. I hear Dan is ill in bed. I hear Sid is ill, too. He has a bad pain in his ribs.
24. One eye is red. Don't use it.
25. It is late. I'll "hit the hay."

## LESSON 16

Short O — hot

### 1

| road | - | ro*a*d | = | rod |
| soap | - | so*a*p | = | sop |
| note | - | not*e* | = | not |
| sole | - | sol*e* | = | Sol |
| hope | - | hop*e* | = | hop |

### 2

| tote | - | tot*e* | = | tot |
| pope | - | pop*e* | = | pop |
| robe | - | rob*e* | = | rob |
| mope | - | mop*e* | = | mop |
| dole | - | dol*e* | = | doll |

## LESSON 16—(Continued)

## DRILL

| on | loll | off | odd |
|---|---|---|---|
| son | lot | rod | toss |
| Tom | not | nod | doll |
| mop | Sol | rot | dot |
| rob | hot | pop | top |
| pot | tot | sob | hop |
| lop | hod | don | Bob |
| sot | doff | moss | sop |
| pod | sod | moth | fob |

*Non-Phonic:* does done some none both of
*Exceptions:* or for

## EXERCISES

1. My name is Sol and his name is Bob. Sol and Bob are pals. Both Sol and Bob are lads.
2. This tot's name is Tom. Tom has a top.
3. Mae has a doll. The doll has on a hat.
4. See the doll hop? See the doll nod?
5. Anne made a pot of hot tea. Anne's dad sips the tea. Lynn had some. Syd had none.
6. It is a hot day to-day. I'll toss off my hat.
7. I feel hot. So does Rod. Sol does not feel hot.
8. He is on top of the hill. I see him there.
9. One day Sol fell off the top of the hill.
10. He fell in a pit. He is ill. I hear him sob.
11. He said if I don't see him home, he may die.
12. I ran to tell his dad. His dad is not home.

## LESSON 16—(Continued)

13. I'll see if Dot is in. No, Dot is not in.
14. The heat is on there. The heat is off here.
15. Don has his hat on. Sol has his hat off.
16. This tot is that man's son. His name is Bob.
17. Bob bit his lip. It pains him a lot.
18. The maid has a mop. I use the maid's mop.
19. Beth made some beef for me. This is for Pete or May.

## LESSON 17

Short U — up

### 1

| use  | - | us¢  | = | us   |
| mute | - | mut¢ | = | mutt |
| tube | - | tub¢ | = | tub  |
| mule | - | mul¢ | = | mull |

### 2

| fuse | - | fus¢ | = | fuss |
| dune | - | dun¢ | = | dun  |
| muse | - | mus¢ | = | muss |
| dude | - | dud¢ | = | dud  |

### DRILL

| us   | pun  | but  | tub  | sub- |
| mud  | up   | butt | bum  | sum  |
| rub  | pup  | puff | muff | mum  |
| hut  | bun  | buff | lull | bus  |
| dub  | hub  | mull | pus  | buss |
| thud | hum  | fun  | run  | thus |
| dull | nun  | bud  | nut  | fuss |
| putt | muss | rut  | sun  | hull |

## LESSON 17—(Continued)

### EXERCISES

1. I had lots of fun to-day at the bay.
2. Bud and I had a bus ride. Then he and I had a sun bath up on top of the hill.
3. On the bus I met a man. He sat in a seat.
4. By the man sat his son. He ate some nuts.
5. This is a nut. I eat nuts.
6. I see Syd. I see Tom, but I don't see Bud.
7. Bud fell in the mud near his home.
8. "I'll lie in the sun," he said.
9. It is hot to sit in the sun.
10. The maid made us some hot buns. Nuts are on top of them.
11. I ate one bun. Tim ate one bun.
12. Bud had nine buns. Sol hid ten buns.
13. I am up at nine a.m. I am in bed at ten p.m.
14. Bud is up on the top of the hill.
15. Bill sees Bud on the top of the hill, so he runs up there to him.
16. I hear him say, "The sun is not so hot up here."
17. Then I run up there to them.
18. There is a hut on the top of the hill near the road.
19. A man sits in the hut.
20. The man has a mule. He lets us ride the mule.
21. A tub is made to bathe in. Some tubs are made of tin.
22. A pup is a dog. My pup's name is Red Tail.

# LESSON 18

**K k**

| | | | | |
|---|---|---|---|---|
| bake | sake | beak | dike | poke |
| lake | make | seek | pike | duke |
| fake | keep | peak | Ike | luke |
| rake | keel | peek | Mike | eke |
| take | keen | kite | oak | meek |
| kid | kiss | hike | Kim | kit |
| kin | leak | like | soak | Ken |

*Non-Phonic:* key
*Abbreviations:* Mr. Mrs. Ms.

## EXERCISES

1. Mr. Duke bakes pies. He pays Ike and Mike to bake pies, too.
2. Mr. Duke likes Ike a lot.
3. Ike is keen and Mike is dull but meek.
4. They are pals, but not kin.
5. Ike likes to poke fun at Mike and kid him.
6. Ken rides up the pike near the lake.
7. He has to ride there on his bike. Some-times he has no bike.
8. Some-times the bike has a leak in the tire.
9. Then he has to hike up the pike.
10. Kim rakes the lanes.
11. I'll be on a hike to-day. I'll take my kit.
12. This is my kit. I put meat in the kit to eat.
13. Ken said he'll meet me here at nine a.m.
14. I see him on the peak of the road.

## LESSON 18—(Continued)

15. I hike ten miles. I see a lake. I dip my feet in the lake.
16. I soak my feet, and then I bathe in the lake. Ken bathes in the lake, too.
17. The lake is deep. There is a hut on the hill near the lake.
18. A man keeps the hut neat. He has a key to the hut.
19. There is an oak by the hut.
20. Mrs. Kidd sits by the oak near a fire.
21. I see Mr. Kidd poke the fire.
22. Kim puts a pan on the fire and bakes the meat.
23. Then Mr. and Mrs. Kidd, Kim, and I eat the meat.
24. Ms. Keane keeps the red bike at the lake.

## LESSON 19

**C c**

c = k  (The hard sound of C)  ck = k

| 1 | | | 2 | | | 3 | | |
|---|---|---|---|---|---|---|---|---|
| cane | - | can | bake | - | back | seek | - | sick |
| cape | - | cap | lake | - | lack | pike | - | pick |
| coat | - | cot | take | - | tack | like | - | lick |
| code | - | cod | sake | - | sack | soak | - | sock |
| cute | - | cut | rake | - | rack | poke | - | pock |
| cube | - | cub | peak | - | peck | duke | - | duck |
| kite | - | kit | dike | - | Dick | luke | - | luck |
| keen | - | ken | beak | - | beck | make | - | Mack |

## LESSON 19—(Continued)

## DRILL

| cane | cat  | peck  | hack | rock |
| cake | cab  | deck  | pack | lock |
| case | cob  | thick | tick | suck |
| coal | cop  | nick  | kick | buck |
| cone | cup  | sick  | mock | tuck |
| cure | neck | Dick  | dock | tyke |

*Non-Phonic:* come   kale

## EXERCISES

1. I'll pack my kit. I'll put meat, a can of peas, some beets, and cake in my kit.
2. This key can lock my kit.
3. I'll pick up my kit and put it on my back.
4. Then I'll be off on a hike up the pike.
5. Dick, Nick, and Duke said they'll be here at nine a.m.
6. I see them on the road.
7. Nick has on his cap. Duke has a thick rod. Dick has a sack on his back.
8. I hike ten miles. I see a lake.
9. I take the pack off my back. Then I bathe in the lake.
10. The lake is deep, up to my neck. I say, "Come in, Nick."
11. He runs to the dock, then hops in the lake.
12. He ducks me. I duck him. He and I had a lot of fun that day.
13. Ike likes to hike, too.
14. He likes to bathe in the lake, but he is sick in bed to-day.
15. I make a fire. Kay makes pan-cakes.
16. I eat the pan-cakes. Rick eats the meat.
17. "I'll make some tea," the man said. So he did. He made tea.

## LESSON 19—(Continued)

18. I had a cup of tea. The man had a cup of tea, too.
19. I can read. Mike can read.
20. This is a cab man. His name is Mack. He has on a cap.
21. He has on a thin coat. He came to take us home.
22. Ann can bake cakes. I like the cakes Ann bakes.
23. There is a rat. The cat sees the rat. The cat kills the rat.
24. There is a hut near an oak on the hill.
25. A man sits on a rock at the oak near a fire.
26. The man pokes the fire. I run up the hill to meet the man.
27. I say, "Hi!" The man says, "Hi, son!"
28. He takes a thin pan. He puts fat in the pan.
29. Then he puts the pan on the fire, but he sees that the pan leaks, so he takes the pan off the fire.
30. The cat sees the fat in the pan. The cat licks it up.
31. The man takes a pot. He puts a duck in the pot.
32. He puts a thick top on the pot. Then he puts it on the fire. He bakes a can of beans, too.
33. "Come in the hut," the man said to me. "Let us eat."
34. He cut the duck. I pick the meat off the bones and eat it. I suck the bones, too.
35. I had meat, kale, beans, and pie. The cat ate the duck's neck.
36. Duke had on a thick coat. He said, "I feel hot. It is hot to-day."
37. I said, "Take off that thick coat." He said, "May-be it is this coat that makes me feel so hot."
38. I toss the bones to the cat. The cat licks the bones.
39. Mike kicks the cat. I hate to see him kick the cat.
40. I tell him not to be rude to the cat.
41. He made a coal fire. I tell him not to do it, but he does it.
42. They don't need a coal fire to-day.

# LESSON 20

**J j**

| Jeb  | Joe  | John | jade |
|------|------|------|------|
| Jake | Jed  | job  | jam  |
| Jane | June | jot  | jeer |
| jail | Jack | Jill | jut  |
| Jean | Jan  | jet  | jab  |
| Joan | Jeff | juke | jeep |
| joke | Jim  | jell | Jay  |
| jute | jibe | jib  | jape |

## EXERCISES

1. This is John. John has a son. His name is Jake.
2. Jan is a fine lad. He has some jam. He eats the jam at one p.m.
3. Jean and Jill like to joke. They take Jake's jam and hide it near the hill.
4. The peak of the hill juts up.
5. Jane and Joan make jam. The jam has to jell.
6. It is a hot day in June, but the jam can jell if it is not in the sun.
7. Jim has a job at the jail. He rides there in a jeep.
8. He sees Jake and John. They jeer at him. John jabs him in the eye, so Jim locks John in jail.
9. He jots their names on the pad.
10. It is hot here in June, so Jane packs up.
11. Mr. and Mrs. Jeff Doak and Jane ride to the lake.
12. Joe meets them at the lake in a jeep.
13. Joe is the son of Mr. and Mrs. Jeff Doak.
14. The dock juts in-to the lake. Joe and Jane hop off the dock. They say it is fun.
15. They eat at one p.m. They eat peas, meat, and jam and sip their tea.
16. Jack and Jill ride in a jeep. Jack likes Jill. Jill's eyes are like jet.

## LESSON 20—(Continued)

17. Jack tells Jill a joke. Jill likes the joke and jots it on the pad.
18. Jill tells the joke to Mr. John Roane.
19. This is a jail. If a man is bad, they lock him in jail.
20. That is no joke.
21. There is Jim, "the bad man," in jail. It is no fun to be in jail.

## LESSON 21

### G g

### (The hard sound of G)

| gait | God | bag | gap | peg |
| gate | go | beg | fig | pig |
| game | gag | big | fog | pug |
| gain | gas | bog | keg | mug |
| gale | get | bug | jig | sag |
| gay | got | hug | jug | nag |
| gear | gum | dig | lag | rag |
| goal | gun | dog | leg | rig |
| goat | hag | dug | log | rug |
| goes | hog | egg | lug | tag |
| gull | jog | gape | cog | tug |

*Non-Phonic: gone*

### EXERCISES

1. John has ten big hens. The hens lay eggs.
2. He puts the eggs in a bag and then takes the bag of eggs to Jim.
3. He sells the eggs at a big gain.

43

## LESSON 21—(Continued)

4. Jim has a job. He makes big rag rugs. His goal is to make fine rugs.
5. Jack meets Jake at the gate. A log lies near the gate.
6. They go to see Joe. They tell him a joke. A gag is a joke, too.
7. Gus is sick in bed. He has a peg leg.
8. He has a lame gait, but he is game and is not sad.
9. Joe's dad takes some logs and rigs up a bed.
10. Jill makes tea and fills the jug. Jill takes the jug of tea to Joe.
11. Joan made Gail a rag doll. The rag doll's gay red hat sags. The doll has a pug nose. Gail hugs the rag doll.
12. Jean likes Joan. Joan does not nag.
13. Jane packs a bag and goes home in June. Jane lugs the bag.
14. Joe has gone to get some eggs, gum, and figs. He got a big mug, too.
15. He'll be home by nine if he gets some gas for his jeep. The jeep is in gear.
16. Gail likes to jog. Gail does not jog in the fog.
17. Mr. Joe Kyle met Mrs. Jack Dunn. "This is my big son John," Mrs. Dunn said.
18. Mr. James sells a bag of figs and some gum to Mrs. Jones.
19. Jake has ten goats. The goats eat hay. The goats eat oats.
20. Gus has ten pigs. A pig is a hog. A pig has a pug nose.
21. There are bugs in the mud. The pig digs a big hole in the mud and eats the bugs.
22. Jim has a gun at home on the rack.
23. Jim's Dad takes his gun and the dog. He goes up the hill.
24. There are cut logs on the hill.
25. He sees a deer. Off goes the gun. Then he hit a gull, too.
26. There is a fog so thick on the hill that Jim's Dad can-not see. Then a big gale comes up, so he and the dog come back home.
27. The dog begs for bones. He dug a hole and hid the bones near the log on the hill.
28. Jane tags Joe. Then Joe tags Peg. It is a tag game and it is fun.
29. Jeff does not tag Joe. He lags.
30. Then they tug at the rope. That is a game, too.

# LESSON 22

## W w

| wade | weep | wife | well | win |
| way  | woke | wipe | wet  | won |
| weed | wait | wise | web  | wick |
| week | wake | wire | wit  | wig |
| weak | wide | wag  | with | we |
| woe  | wale | wile | waif | wane |
| wean | wine | wed  | will | wail |

*Non-Phonic:* won't

## EXERCISES

1. John has a dog. The dog wags its tail. He is wise.
2. He waits near John's bed.
3. John's wife woke him up at nine a.m. John wakes up and wipes his eyes.
4. John and his wife take the dog to the lake with them. On the way, they see weeds near the road.
5. The lake is wide. John and the dog wade in the lake. They get wet.
6. In their kit is a thick rag. John wipes his wet feet with it. Then his wife wipes the wet dog with the same rag.
7. Jeff wed Jane in June. He wed Jane on a wet day.
8. Jeff is weak and sick. He has lain in bed a week.
9. I'll wire his wife Jane to come home. Jane gets the wire and weeps.
10. Jane is a wise wife and will come home with Jeff's Dad. They won't wait.
11. Jane ran up the wide lane to their home with their bags.
12. Jeff woke up. Jane will wait on him and will make him some cake, too.

## LESSON 22—(Continued)

13. He likes the way Jane bakes cake. He will get well.
14. We will go with Gail and Peg to the big game this week.
15. They will wait at the gate near the well.
16. We will meet them there, and then we will be on the way.
17. We won't win if we don't tag them.
18. They use their wits, but their will to win is weak, so we win.
19. They won the game in May, but we won the game in June.
20. There is a cob-web on the pane. The wise wife will wet the rag and wipe the cob-web off the pane with it.
21. The hot days are on the wane.
22. To make a fire, we will need a wide wick. If we don't get a wick, we won't get heat.
23. John's wife will wean their son Jim. He weeps and wails, but he is big and can eat with them.
24. Jill put a wig on the rag doll. The doll's hat is red as wine.
25. Jill will make Jean's doll a wig and will take it to Jean this week.
26. There are weeds and a deep well near the wide road near Jake's home.
27. There are wires on the poles on the wide road.
28. The weeds are in the way, so Jake and his wife dig them up.

## LESSON 23

### V v

| vain | vine | Dave | rave | dive |
| vane | veep | vat | save | vim |
| vale | vote | rove | wave | eve |
| vase | van | cave | waive | leave |
| veal | vie | gave | five | weave |
| veer | jive | vet | eaves | vise |
| vile | cove | pave | hive | heave |

*Short Vowel Before V:* give   have   love
*Vowel Before V Both Long and Short:*   live   dove
*Non-Phonic:*   vein   veil

46

## LESSON 23—(Continued)

## EXERCISES

1. We live here. They'll pave the road near the home we live in.
2. Dave does not feel well.
3. I got up at five to give him a pill. He says the pill is vile.
4. I made fire. There are live coals in it.
5. Then I gave Dave some tea. He did not take it, so I will save it.
6. He is in pain. The pain leaves and Dave sips the tea, so I did not save it in vain.
7. Dave gave Jill a neat vase. It has vines and leaves on its sides.
8. The vase came in a van at five p.m.
9. We sit on a rock near the cove and weave.
10. We see a bee hive. We love to see the bees go in the hole of the hive.
11. Dave said one day this week he will take me on a hike.
12. I wait one day in vain. I wait five days, but he does not come, so I give up hope.
13. To-day he came to tell me that we will leave at five a.m.
14. My dog loves to go on a hike with me.
15. I feel some-one poke me in my side.
16. I wake up and see it's Vic. He wags his tail.
17. "Well, well!" I said. "That's fine! You did not wake me in vain. I have to get up."
18. I got up. I ate eggs. I gave Vic a big bone. I love Vic.
19. By then Dave came. "It is five," Dave said.
20. I pack veal, peas, jam, and cake in my kit.
21. I put on the thick coat my Dad gave me. I take my cap.

## LESSON 23—(Continued)

22. Vic lay at my feet. He begs me to let him go with us, so I give in.
23. I wave to him. He leaps. We go. We leave on the dot.
24. We rove in the vale. We see a dove.
25. We dive in the lake. We heave a rock in-to the lake.
26. We have no luck. There came a gale, then the rain.
27. We are wet, so we vote to go home.
28. "We will have to go back," Dave said, so we leave.
29. But my dog Vic is wise. He led us to a cave.
30. We rave that Vic is so wise.
31. We have to wait till a bus will pass here.
32. If we ride back home on the bus, we will save time.
33. We had to wait for the bus till five p.m.
34. A bus came. We live near the main line. We got home late.

## LESSON 24

### Y y
(Y as a consonant)

| Yale | yen | year | yoke | Yule | yon |
| yell | yap | yes | yet | yams | yo-yo |

*Non-Phonic:* you  yak
*Exceptions:* youth  your  yours
*Contractions:* you're  you'll  you've

# LESSON 24—(Continued)

## EXERCISES

1. I like yams. Do you? We bake the yams and eat them hot.
2. Yale's Mom made a deep yoke in my coat. The yoke makes the coat fit well.
3. Yale is a youth in his teen years.
4. Yale has a dog. His name is Vic.
5. It is not yet a year that Mr. Wells gave Vic to Yale at Yule time.
6. Yale lives in Maine. Yes, Yale is a fine youth.
7. I have not seen Yale in years. I am on my way to see Yale to-day.
8. "Hi, Mrs. Lee! I hope you are well. Is Yale in? May I see him?"
9. "Yes, he is in, but he is in bed yet. I'll wake him up."
10. "Jim, are you here? Dear, O dear! Come in, Jim," I hear him yell.
11. He is off the bed. "Put on your bath-robe," his Mom yells to him.
12. With one leap Yale is near me.
13. "I hope you feel well," I said.
14. "I am well. I hope you're the same."
15. "Did you see the kite I made this year?"
16. "Yes, I did. It is a fine kite you made. Mine is not as big as yours. Do you have a yo-yo?"
17. "Is your Dad home?" "Yes, he is. I'll tell him you are here."
18. "Dad, Oh, Dad! Jim is here!" "Well, well! That's fine," Dad yells back.
19. "I have to go. I leave at five p.m. It has been fine to see you and your Mom and Dad."
20. "Oh, do not go yet. I have not seen you in years."

# LESSON 25

## Two Consonants at the End of a Word

back − c̸ + n = ba**n**k
(Spelling ck follows short vowel:
"n" you hear takes place of "c")
Step 1:  b  a  c  k
Step 2:  b  a  c̸  k (− c)
Step 3:  b  a  n  k  (+ n)

tac**k** − k̸ + t = tac**t**
(Spelling ck follows short vowel:
"t" you hear takes place of "k")
Step 1:  t  a  c  k
Step 2:  t  a  c  k̸ (− k)
Step 3:  t  a  c  t  (+ t)

### Short A

| bank | thank | lamp  | act   | pang |
| band | sank  | land  | tank  | pant |
| damp | hand  | bang  | sand  | pact |
| gang | camp  | sang  | hang  | cask |
| fact | rang  | mask  | cast  | rapt |
| task | tact  | last  | caste | fang |
| raft | fast  | can't | mast  | yank |
| ask  | and   | ant   | past  | ramp |
| vast | rank  | valve | apt   | vamp |
| lapse| dank  | gasp  | bask  | rasp |

### Long A

waist    paint    faint    saint

*Non-Phonic:*  waste   haste   paste   baste   taste

## LESSON 25—(Continued)

## EXERCISES

1. The mud is deep up to my waist.
2. This is my waist line.
3. This is red paint. I can paint well.
4. They paint the raft with red paint.
5. I'll paint my boat and the pole, too, with the same paint, so I won't waste it.
6. Yale feels faint. "Don't faint, dear."
7. I come home at five. I take off my hat and coat.
8. I hang my hat and coat on a rack.
9. It is a fact that I go to camp to-day. John and I leave at five p.m.
10. Yale can go with us, too. Yale is a Yank.
11. The camp is on the bank of the lake.
12. Near the camp is a sand hill.
13. The ants live in the ant hills on the sand hill.
14. There is a boat at sea. The boat has a mast and a sail.
15. We sail the boat fast past the raft. Then we land. We then cast a net.
16. Mrs. Kell will baste the meat and then taste it.
17. Last year a boat sank in the lake near the camp.
18. I have a big task to do yet. I have to pack my kit and bag.
19. I will have to act fast, as it is late. "Haste makes waste."
20. Some-one rang the bell. I hear some-one bang at the gate.
21. I can't go. I can't see. We have no lamp.
22. It is the gang. They are no saints. They came with a band.
23. There is John. I'll ask him to give me a hand.
24. "Thank you, John. You did a lot."
25. "Let us eat," he said. "Taste the pie."
26. We ate and we sang and we had a fine time.
27. There is a cask of wine near the last ramp.

# LESSON 26

## Two Consonants at the End of a Word

### Short E

| | | | | |
|---|---|---|---|---|
| kept | left | bend | belt | lent |
| end | tend | help | weld | delve |
| desk | dent | best | yelp | dense |
| jest | lend | self | tent | elf |
| held | melt | bent | tenth | elk |
| nest | pest | mend | send | fend |
| rest | test | pelt | rent | sense |
| wept | west | went | sent | sect |
| felt | vest | lest | else | helm |
| vend | depth | wend | theft | vent |

### Long E

| | | | | |
|---|---|---|---|---|
| east | least | beast | yeast | feast |

## EXERCISES

1. The East Side team meets here day by day.
2. I live in the East End. They live in the West End.
3. We have a feast at least one day in the month.
4. That beast is tame. Mules are beasts.
5. Ted buys oats and hay to feed the beasts.
6. Here I am at last in Camp Lee. I went to camp last year, too.
7. We left home June the tenth at five a.m., and we got here at ten p.m.
8. We set up a tent. Ned held the net for us.
9. We have a cot and a desk in the tent.
10. We sit on the cot at the desk and read.

# LESSON 26—(Continued)

11. Yale, Dave, Jake, and Van came to-day.
12. John and I will help them set up a tent.
13. I'll mend the hole in the tent. I'll tend to that my-self in the best way.
14. I'll do that fast, or else I'll be late to bed. I need a rest.
15. We sent Van to get some ham, meat, buns, cakes, eggs, yeast, and a hen. He has gone way up to the West End to get them.
16. I see it is one p.m. and he is not back yet.
17. So I went to ask Dave to lend us a hand.
18. Dave said that he came here to take a rest. Jake said he felt bad.
19. Yale said he can't help us. He has to take a test.
20. I see that we can't get help. I went and made a fire.
21. John said, "You tend to the fire, and I'll do my best. I'll do the rest."
22. By then Van came back with the ham and eggs.
23. We had a fine meal, thank God.
24. To aid means to help. To help means to lend a hand.
25. I'll read and add, so I can pass my test by the tenth.
26. I'll get that done, and then I'll help Ben.
27. Beth, I'll lend you my pen. See that you don't bend the end.
28. My Dad sent me that pen last May the tenth.
29. There are ten red hens. They eat less than the rest. They eat the least.
30. Mike has sense. He feeds the hens to make them fat and then he sells them.
31. Ben said to pay the rent. Tell Ben I'll pay the rent by the tenth.

# LESSON 27

## Two Consonants at the End of a Word

### Short I

| lift  | fist  | lint  | kink  | list |
| tilt  | wing  | think | lisp  | mint |
| ring  | sink  | silk  | mist  | sift |
| wink  | kilt  | gift  | rift  | limp |
| sing  | disk  | hint  | rinse | ilk  |
| pink  | mink  | ink   | rink  | film |
| bilk  | fifth | silt  | wilt  | hilt |
| thing | risk  | imp   | link  | filth |
| milk  | jilt  | tint  | king  | gild |

Non-Phonic: pint  ninth  build  built  kiln  disc

## EXERCISES

1. Mrs. King can sing well. Yale, can you sing? Let us hear you sing.
2. This is Mr. Jeff King. Mr. King sells milk and eggs.
3. He has a big jug of milk in his left hand.
4. He takes it to the camp to sell.
5. Mr. King can't go fast, as he limps. He has a cane in one hand.
6. I think I'll lend him a hand and give him a lift.
7. He said, "No, thank you. You can't lift that big jug of milk." "Yes, I can," I said.
8. "Well, well! That is fine, but don't tilt it."
9. I hear Tim limps, too. He fell in the rink.
10. Here is a list of things I need: a bag of nuts, one ham, one fat hen, hot buns, and a pint of milk.
11. I'll buy a thin tin pan, too. I'll rinse it and then I'll use it.

## LESSON 27—(Continued)

12. There is a list of names I'll send gifts to.
13. "Let me see that list." "Here it is. Read it."
14. I'll send a ring to Tom. He is my best pal.
15. I will send a pink tie to Sol. I'll send fine silk hose to Ann, and I'll send a mink coat to Kate.
16. It will take a mint to get these things. Yet I'll do it. I love to give.
17. "I'll give you a ring." "Do you mean a real ring as a gift?" "No, I mean I'll ring your bell."
18. I had to use the kiln for the gift I made.
19. Bill fell in a deep pit, and Bim had to lift him up in-to his bed. He says he has a pain in his hips.
20. He feels pain in his feet and hands, too.
21. He is so thin you can see his ribs. His nose, lips, and eyes are red as beets.
22. I'll give him a pill. I'll sit here till ten p.m. and read to him. This is the ninth day he has been sick.

## LESSON 28

### Two Consonants at the End of a Word

#### Short O

| boss | loss | cost | long | month |
| song | lost | fond | soft | gong |
| opt | pond | golf | loft | solve |
| bond | moss | toss | monk | moth |
| tongs | font | pomp | thong | honk |

#### Long O

coast    boast    roast    toast

## LESSON 28—(Continued)

## EXERCISES

1. There goes my dad's boss. My dad's boss is fond of me, and I am fond of him. Fond means to like.
2. My boss is a sad man. He lost his son.
3. My boss' son died last year. A year is not a long time, yet it seems long.
4. My boss gave me this ring last year.
5. I bet a ring like that costs a lot.
6. Jim had a ring like this one. His dad gave it to him, but he lost it in the pond.
7. He may have lost it in the moss up on the hill.
8. "It is not the cost of the thing," he says, "but it is the loss of the gift that makes me feel so bad."
9. It is a long, long way to go to get to John and Joan.
10. They live on the hill in the West End.
11. Joan and John sing songs well, but John boasts a lot.
12. We went to see Jean and Jack, too. They live on the sea-coast.
13. Jean made us roast beef and Jack made the toast.
14. I like roast beef on rye.
15. One day Tom said to Sol, "This is one of those hot days of this month. Some days of this month are so hot that one roasts."
16. "Let's hop in the pond. Let's bathe."
17. At the pond they met Bob. Bob is Dan Hope's son, and Dan Hope is Tom's boss. Sol and Bob are fond of Tom.
18. Bob sat near the pond on the damp, soft sand with a rod in his hand.
19. Sol said, "Bob, if you don't hop in, I'll toss you in!"
20. "Is that so? No, you won't!"
21. There is my big Dane in the soft moss on the hill.
22. I'll yell to him to come back to me.
23. Did you buy a U.S. bond to-day?
24. Yale buys a bond on the tenth day of the month.
25. Don lost one of his bonds in the loft. That is odd, is it not?
26. You solve that loss. But Don has some bonds left.

# LESSON 29

## Two Consonants at the End of a Word

### Short U

| jump | rust | bump | punk | mumps |
| junk | hump | lump | husk | rump |
| tusk | dusk | lung | hunk | sulk |
| hung | must | runt | bust | sung |
| dust | hunt | bulk | rung | pulp |
| just | sunk | lust | pulse | duct |
| dump | gust | pump | bunk | gulp |
| thump | tuft | bulb | dunk | fund |

*Exceptions:* bull  pull  full  put

## EXERCISES

1. A tube is a long pipe. They use a test tube to test things in.
2. The cat jumps at the rat. To leap is to jump.
3. The cat hunts rats. To get rid of rats have a cat in your home.
4. Men hunt deer, bulls, and ducks.
5. To hunt deer one must have a gun. Get rid of the rust on your gun.
6. Use lots of soap and rub it on your hands.
7. John said he will go on a deer hunt.
8. You must not hunt in May and June.
9. I must have a dog. One of my dogs is just a runt. One can't run.
10. He limps and one is sick. He got hit. He yelps.
11. He has a big lump on his leg. The lump is as big as my fist.
12. I'll ask Mr. Funk to lend me his gun and dog.
13. Near the hut on the hill is a pump. A man is in the hut. The man built the hut.

## LESSON 29—(Continued)

14. He hunts deer, elk, and ducks. He says it is a lot of fun to hunt.
15. Bud fell in a rut full of mud. Mr. Dunn ran to pull him up and help him.
16. Mr. Dunn felt Bud's pulse. He felt his hands and feet.
17. Then he said, "I feel a lump on your left hand, and I see a bump on your nose and a hump on your back."
18. "I'll tie up the lump on your hand. Then I'll send you home, but you must not rub the bump on your nose or the hump on your back."
19. Bud must not ride on a bus by him-self. He must not run fast. If he does, he puffs.
20. Bud must sit at home, and that is no fun. He says, "It is a dull day."
21. I like to jump rope. Joe, can you jump?
22. Yes, but I hate to jump in the dust.
23. The dust gets in my lungs and makes me sick.
24. This is a junk pile. Things we can't use are junk.
25. We put tin cans and pots and pans that leak in the junk pile.
26. We'll build a home near the gulf.

# LESSON 30

**Sh sh**

## Read across

shade - shad    shake - shack    shame - sham

## Read down

| shape | sheen | shift | ship  | dish   |
| shave | shall | shaft | shod  | wish   |
| leash | shank | ash   | shot  | rush   |
| sheaf | hush  | cash  | shop  | shun   |
| sheet | shine | dash  | shock | shuck  |
| sheep | shin  | hash  | mash  | shut   |
| shear | shell | rash  | sash  | she    |
| sheer | shelf | gush  | fish  | sheath |
| mush  | shag  | shed  | shy   | sheathe |

*Short Vowel Before V:* shove
*Non-Phonic:* sure   shoe
*Exceptions:* bush   push

## EXERCISES

1. A shad is a fish. Shad makes a fine dish.
2. This is a buck shad and that is a roe shad.
3. An eel is a fish and so is a pike.
4. This is a shoe shine shop. I need a shoe shine.
5. These shoes need soles. This shoe needs a heel.

## LESSON 30—(Continued)

6. This is a sheep and this is a goat.
7. They shear sheep, but they do not shear goats.
8. Don't shove and push me. It is rude to act that way.
9. I'll aim at the can. That will be a sure hit.
10. I feel sure I can win the game.
11. A ship is a boat. A ship sails the seas.
12. A ship sank just off the coast.
13. There is the shack Mr. Sheer built on the top of that hill near the shed.
14. Mr. Sheer lives in the shack by him-self.
15. Mr. Sheer has a full beard. He does not shave.
16. He sits on a big rock near a bush in the shade.
17. By his feet is a dog. He keeps the dog on a leash.
18. Shall I yell to him? Shall I wake him up?
19. "Hush, John, hush! Shut up!" I said. "You may shock him. It is a shame to wake up the man."
20. We came near the shack. We shake hands with Mr. Sheer.
21. He gave us a dish full of fish and some hash.
22. He got the dish off the shelf in the shack.
23. We ate. Then John said, "It is late. We shall have to rush, or else we shall miss the bus."
24. "Don't go yet," Mr. Sheer said. "Don't rush."
25. "But it is five p.m., and we must leave."
26. "Well, then, so be it," Mr. Sheer said. "I wish you luck."
27. Then we left the shack. I am sure we shall be back.
28. You may be sure of that. That is a sure thing.
29. Are you sure of that? No one can be sure.
30. I am sure she can do it. Just wait and see.
31. Sure, we shine and mend shoes here. Sheen means shine.
32. Sure, we sell men's shoes here in this shop.
33. Don't shove your feet in your shoes. Just ease them on.
34. She is shy, but she sells shoes in the shoe shop.

# LESSON 31

**Ch**  **ch**

| Column 1 | | Column 2 | |
|---|---|---|---|
| chafe - chaff | | reach - retch | |
| cheap - chip | | peach - pitch | |

| | | | | |
|---|---|---|---|---|
| chain | chaff | hatch | beach | lunch |
| chafe | chat | catch | teach | filch |
| chase | chant | fetch | peach | finch |
| cheap | check | ditch | reach | pinch |
| cheer | chest | latch | roach | hunch |
| cheek | chess | match | poach | munch |
| cheat | chin | patch | leech | bench |
| cheese | chill | pitch | each | belch |
| chime | chick | itch | coach | chinch |
| chide | chip | witch | botch | chock |
| choke | chop | Dutch | thatch | inch |
| chose | chum | hitch | mulch | batch |
| chap | chunk | notch | fetch | gulch |
| champ | chuck | hutch | bunch | lynch |

*Non-Phonic:* rich   much   such   niche
*Exception:* Butch


## EXERCISES

1. Dutch Long is the coach of the team at the beach.
2. Coach Dutch is a fine chap. He is my chum.
3. Wait and see him go to bat and then catch.
4. To pitch is to toss.

# LESSON 31—(Continued)

5. He said he will teach me the game. I wish I had gone to the beach with him.
6. Butch and Chips are chums. They are on the same team.
7. Coach Lynch is a fine chap, too. He likes to have Butch pitch and Chips catch.
8. One day Coach Lynch said, "I just itch to go to the beach, but lack the funds to get there."
9. "Well," said Butch, "let's hitch-hike. That will make the cost cheap, and we can reach there in time to see the big game."
10. "I have a hunch that if we wait on Champ Road, we will get a lift in no time."
11. "That's it," said Lynch. "Don't just sit there and chide. Come on, let's go!"
12. Off they go to Champ Road. They sit there on the road-side.
13. They wait and wait, but have no such luck as to catch a ride.
14. At last there comes a chap in a red bus.
15. He waves to them to get in. He yells, "Hop in, lads."
16. They rode a mile and then—bang went a tire!
17. They fell in a ditch. Butch cut his chin, Chips had a pain in his chest and had chills, and Lynch had his cheeks cut and felt much pain.
18. By and by, Dutch said, "Cheer up, pals. Keep your chins up!"
19. Well, at last they got to the beach just in time to see the tail end of the game, but there is no bench for them to sit on.

# LESSON 32

**Wh** **wh**

wh = **hw**. (Read **hw**)

| whale | whiff | wheat | whim | wheel | whelp |
| white | whine | while | whack | why | whisk |
| whit | whist | when | whet | whip | whoa |

*Non-Phonic:* w)ho  w)hom  w)hose  w)hole
what  where  which  whey

## EXERCISES

1. On the beach Lynch, Butch, and Chips met the rest of the gang.
2. They did not eat for a whole day. "Who will go to fetch some things to eat?" Lynch said.
3. "I'll tell you what we'll do. Let's each pitch in and one of us will go to fetch them."
4. "But who shall go? Whom shall we send?"
5. "Where shall we buy the things and what shall we get?"
6. "Why this whole fuss?" said Butch. "I'll tell you what I'll do. I'm not as rich as you, so I can't pitch in, but I can go and fetch the things if Joe White will lend me his wheel."
7. "Sure," said Joe White, "you may use my wheel, but I'd like to see it back whole."
8. "Why, I can ride a wheel as well as you can. There is no need to tell me what to do."
9. "Hush, hush!" said Lynch. "Don't you fuss."
10. "Here is a list of the things we need—cheese cake, peach pies, a whole-wheat loaf, eggs, a big chunk of ham, some cheese tid-bits, a jug of milk, and pop."
11. "Rush, Butch. Be gone, and don't be long."

## LESSON 32—(Continued)

12. "Who has a match? While Butch is on his way, we will make a fire on the beach so we can poach the eggs."
13. It is nine, it is ten, but Butch is not back yet.
14. "What keeps him? Where is he? When will we eat?"
15. "Why is he so long? Those eggs will hatch by the time he'll get back with them!"
16. "I bet he has lost my wheel," said Joe White.
17. "Here, each of you has had your say. It's time to act," said Chips.
18. "This is no fun. Butch may be ill on the road. We will have to hunt for him."
19. Just then, while Chips said this, Butch came back with a load of things to eat.
20. They ate and sang. They had a whale of a fine time.

## LESSON 33

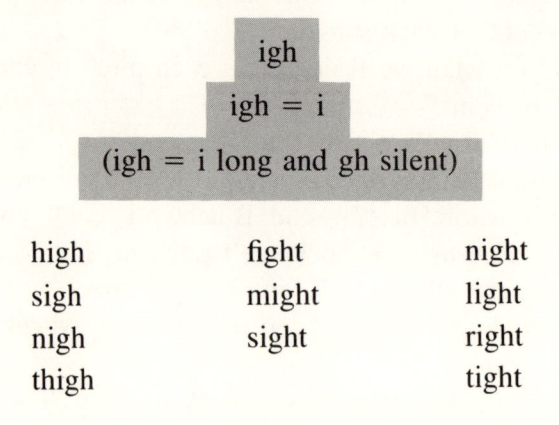

igh
igh = i
(igh = i long and gh silent)

| high | fight | night |
| sigh | might | light |
| nigh | sight | right |
| thigh |  | tight |

### EXERCISES

1. Yale has been up a whole night. He has a job on a night shift.
2. He does not see well. His eye-sight is bad.
3. Tell Yale not to read by a dim light if his eye-sight is bad.

## LESSON 33—(Continued)

4. I think you are right. I will tell him that.
5. Jack reads a lot at night. Some-times he sits up till mid-night.
6. I tell him it is high time to go to bed.
7. He just heaves a deep sigh and says that he has to pass a test and that life is just one long fight.
8. Yes, he is right. We must fight to reach a goal.
9. Jack chose the right road of life.
10. He says, "Give of what you have and don't be tight."
11. One who is tight hates to give, but loves to take.
12. "Right is might," he says, "but might is not right."
13. "Aim high and you might get there," he loves to tell us.
14. He reads while he eats his light lunch, and then he is off in a rush.
15. I ask him to wait, not to rush, and I beg him not to go in the rain.
16. "But time does not wait," he says with a sigh and runs to catch a bus.
17. "It's just a light rain. I won't get wet much," he says.
18. It is high tide. What does high tide mean? It is the time of the day when the seas rise.
19. When the sun shines we have light. "Let there be light."
20. Do and say the right thing at the right time.

## LESSON 34

Qu    qu

(qu = kw. Qu has the sound of kw.)

| quake  | queen  | quite | quit  |
| quaint | queer  | quote | quilt |
| quail  | quest  | quick | quell |
| quack  | quench | quill | quire |

*Non-Phonic:* queue

## LESSON 34—(Continued)

## EXERCISES

1. What is a queen? A queen is the wife of a king.
2. What does quake mean? Quake is the same as shake.
3. Quaint means odd. A duck quacks. Quench means to check. We quench a fire.
4. To quote is to say the same thing some-one else said.
5. John Quinn said, "I have seen Queen Ann"— end of quote.
6. To quit means to give up. Don't quit your job.
7. Quick means fast. To be in quest of means to seek.
8. Mr. Quinn is quite rich. He and his wife live like a king and queen, but they say he is a quaint man.
9. He likes to eat well, but hates to give a bite to those who are in need.
10. One day he went in-to a shop and said that he is in quest of quilts.
11. "Yes," said the man, "we have quilts."
12. "Do you keep thick quilts?" "No," said the man, "we don't keep quilts, we sell them."
13. "Quit your jokes," said Mr. Quinn. "Let me see the best quilt you have."
14. "But," said the man, "what is the big rush, and may I ask why you need a thick quilt on a hot day like this?"
15. "I must be quick. My wife has the chills. Mrs. Quinn is quite sick. She quakes like a leaf."
16. "If that is the case," said the man, "then I shall quit the fun and be quick to wait on you."
17. "I am quite sure this thick quilt will help a lot to make Mrs. Quinn feel at ease."

# LESSON 35

**X x**

(**x** = **ks**. X has the sound of **ks**.)

| ax  | Max  | tax   | wax  | hoax |
| fix | mix  | six   | ox   | sox  |
| box | fox  | pox   | ex-  | text |
| sex | next | sixth | coax | jinx |
| hex | vex  | lax   | Rex  | lynx |

## EXERCISES

1. This is my tin lunch box. Max will fix a key to fit my lunch box so I can lock it.
2. Don't mix your lunch box with mine, as we do not have the same lunch.
3. Max gets up at six a.m. He takes his dog King, his gun, an ax, and his lunch box. He is off on a fox hunt.
4. Last night he came home with one deer and one fox which he had shot.
5. Next time he goes on a fox hunt, I will ask him to let me go with him. I will not have to coax him.
6. Max can box well. To box means to fight.
7. Max and Rex will box next week. It will be the sixth time they will box.
8. Ned Lang said, "Will you come with me? I'll get box seats."
9. A box seat is the best seat. A box seat is a ring-side seat.
10. "Sure I will! You don't have to coax me."
11. "But that is queer. Max can lick six like Rex."
12. "When and where will it be?" "It will be at the Queen Ann on the sixth of next month."
13. Max has a case of pox. The next day Rex has a case of pox, too.

## LESSON 35—(Continued)

14. It seems the pox is a jinx, and it means they will not box on the sixth. This is not a hoax.
15. "Do you fix shoes here?" "Yes, we fix shoes while you wait."
16. "I have six shoes for you to fix. Don't mix them up."
17. "They will make holes in my sox if you don't fix them."
18. "By the way, who will fix my ax?" "The man at the next bench will fix it."
19. We use an ax to chop with. An ax must be keen, or else it will not cut well.
20. My next bill is due on the sixth.
21. I must not be lax. I must pay my tax on time.
22. I'll ask Mr. Tom Mix to wait till the tenth of next month.
23. I'll pay that tax bill by then. It will vex Mr. Mix if I am late.
24. Read your text so you will pass your test.
25. We must quote six lines of the text on this test.
26. Mr. and Mrs. Dix have an ox and a mule. They mix feed for the ox and mule.
27. The mule won't eat the mix Mr. and Mrs. Dix fix for him.
28. I am sure that will vex them.
29. Mr. Dix has a dog, too. The dog's name is Rex, and he is of the male sex.
30. Mrs. Dix is not lax. Mr. Dix does not have to coax Mrs. Dix to do the tasks.
31. She rubs wax on the bench to make it shine.

# LESSON 36

## Z z

| zeal | daze | doze | size |
| Zeke | haze | razz | fuzz |
| zone | gaze | jazz | quiz |
| zip  | maze | fez  | wheeze |
| zest | raze | buzz | fizz |

*Non-Phonic:* zinc

a b c d e f g h i j k l m n o p q r s t u v w x y z

A B C D E F G H I J K L M N O P Q R S T U V W X Y Z

## EXERCISES

1. We had a quiz to-day. To quiz means to ask.
2. Zeke is one of the Quiz Kids.
3. Zeke has big feet. He needs a man's size shoes.
4. What size shoes are these?
5. Zeke likes jazz. Dave does not like jazz.
6. A fez is a cap. Mr. Zinc has on a red fez. Max will fix his fez on just right.
7. This is a safe zone. That is not a safe zone.
8. It is sad that you live in that zone. They will raze your home in that zone.
9. What is that buzz I hear? That's the buzz of the bee.
10. Don't just sit there and gaze at me. Run! Quick!
11. That man, Mr. Zip, is in a daze. He must be ill.
12. He has been in a daze a whole day.
13. Don't just sit there and doze. Go right to bed.
14. You must not gaze at the sun. It will daze you.

## LESSON 36—(Continued)

15. Be sure to wipe the fuzz off the peach. You must not eat the peach fuzz. It may make you sick.
16. If you have a task to do, it will be done fast if you do it with zeal and zest.
17. We coat the pipe with zinc.

## LESSON 37

### Two Separately-Sounded Consonants at the Beginning of a Word

#### Long A

| b-rain | play | trade | state | trait |
| p-lain | pray | grate | scale | flame |
| t-rail | claim | graze | grape | crave |
| snail | drain | bray | plate | stale |
| grave | slain | stay | glaze | snake |
| frame | frail | stain | clay | crane |
| crate | slate | grain | dray | drape |
| brave | slave | braid | slay | craze |
| spade | grade | blame | train | gray |
| plane | flake | blade | praise | sway |
| blaze | scathe | drake | brake | tray |

*Non-Phonic:* skate

## LESSON 37—(Continued)

## EXERCISES

Mr. Gray went to Spain last year. He went by boat and train. He'll stay there till next June. Don't play with fire and don't play with a snake. Play safe, do not skate near a lake. This is a grape vine and that is grape wine. I use a keen blade to shave. If the blade is dull, I can't shave. In this shop, they sell high grade meats. You will like to trade here. Mr. Drake is a big, fat, brave man, but Mrs. Drake is frail. Frail means weak and thin.

We use a spade to dig with. With a spade we dig a hole, a pit, a ditch, and a grave. This is a tray. On the tray is a plate and a cup. On the plate are meat, beets, kale, and a cheese cake, and in the glass is milk. It is Mr. Gray's lunch. Mr. Gray has a clay pipe. Mr. Blake and Mr. Drake live near the state line, where they raise grain and hogs.

If the meat is stale, don't eat it. Stale meat may make you sick. If you hear a mule bray, you may be sure there will be rain. Zeke said, "Let us pray to God to keep us well and let us praise His name."

## LESSON 38

### Two Separately-Sounded Consonants at the Beginning of a Word

#### Short A

| 1 | | | 2 | | | 3 | | |
|---|---|---|---|---|---|---|---|---|
| c-laim | - | c-lam | s-late | - | s-lat | b-rain | - | b-ran |
| plain | - | plan | snake | - | snack | Spain | - | span |
| stake | - | stack | plane | - | plan | glade | - | glad |

71

## LESSON 38—(Continued)

| brag  | drag  | slab  | flag  | slam  |
| stag  | brat  | flap  | slap  | trap  |
| clad  | snap  | flat  | clan  | glad  |
| clap  | grab  | spat  | crab  | stab  |
| snag  | scan  | flax  | staff | scab  |

### Two Consonants at the Beginning and Two at the End of a Word

### Short A

| black  | crack  | clash  | flask  | grand  |
| tramp  | brand  | drank  | graft  | smack  |
| flank  | grass  | stand  | thrash | cramp  |
| stamp  | blank  | clasp  | frank  | plant  |
| class  | glass  | slack  | track  | blast  |
| grasp  | trash  | crank  | draft  | grant  |
| craft  | flash  | plank  | slang  | branch |
| prank  | slant  | tract  | crash  | gland  |
| clank  | spank  | clamp  | smash  | snack  |
| grasps | crass  | scamp  | bland  | clasps |

*Non-Phonic: plaid*
*Exception: flak*

### EXERCISES

This is my flag, the flag of my land. Miss Flax will teach the class a hand craft. A hand craft means a trade. Miss Flax will teach us to draft and to plant. To draft means to make plans. The class rules are: "**Don't** slam things on the desk. Don't stamp and don't drag your

## LESSON 38—(Continued)

feet. Don't play pranks. Use no slang. Keep off the grass. Don't be a crank. Be brave but do not brag. Don't smack your lips when you eat."

"See that man, Mrs. Black?" "Yes, Mrs. White. Why do you ask?" "I think he is a tramp—no shave, no shoes, and clad in rags." "I just hate to see a man in such a state." "I don't blame him. He must be weak from the way he drags his feet. I bet he did not eat to-day." "I'd be glad to help you, my dear man. Here, take this and get a hot meal. A plate of meat and a glass of milk will fix you up." "Thanks," said the tramp, and in a flash he had gone to have his lunch. He ate and drank and then he felt grand, he said.

Frank set the rat trap. He put cheese as bait to catch the rats. When the rat comes to eat the cheese, the trap goes off with a snap. Don't put hot things in a glass. It may crack.

## LESSON 39

**Two Separately-Sounded Consonants at the Beginning of a Word**

**Long E**

| | | | |
|---|---|---|---|
| clean | dream | sneak | clear |
| cream | steal | steam | treat |
| speak | plead | spear | smear |
| pleat | plea | grease | freak |
| breach | flea | crease | bleach |
| preach | breathe | bleak | please |
| bleed | greet | sweep | steel |
| sweet | sleeve | creep | green |
| sleep | speed | three | tree |

73

# LESSON 39—(Continued)

| creed | fleet | flee | free |
| freed | greed | Greek | sleet |
| steed | steep | steer | speech |
| Steve | breeze | sneeze | freeze |
| creek | creak | tweed | bleat |

## EXERCISES

I go to class at nine and come home at three. Steve and I help to keep the home clean. We have no steam heat in the flat in which we live. Steve has to fix the fire in the grate, or else we'd freeze. I sweep and dust and make the beds. Then I am free to play till six. Three and three make six. At six we eat and at ten we go to sleep. On a clear day, we play on the green grass, and when it rains, we stay at home as we do not like to get wet. If your feet get wet, you sneeze and can't breathe well. When I come home, I greet Mom and Dad, and when I go to sleep, I say, "Sweet dreams."

Mr. Green will speak to us to-day. Mr. Fleet will ask him to give us a speech. To hear Mr. Green preach is a real treat. "Will you please tell me where Mrs. Spear lives?" "Sure, my dear, Mrs. Spear lives on the top of that steep hill right by those two big trees. You will like the clean, clear breeze up there, but do not speed on the sleet."

To steal is to rob. We must not steal, but we may use steel. Steel is used to make a lot of things. "Steve, can you speak Greek?" "Yes I can." "Will you please teach me to speak and read Greek?" "Yes, I'll be glad to do that." "Thank you!"

# LESSON 40

### Two Separately-Sounded Consonants at the Beginning of a Word

#### Short E

| 1 | | | 2 | | |
|---|---|---|---|---|---|
| bleed | - | bled | steep | - | step |
| breed | - | bred | speed | - | sped |
| steam | - | stem | sleep | - | slept |
| creep | - | crept | flee | - | fled |

| stet | glen | dreg | flex | when |
|------|------|------|------|------|
| shred | sled | then | fret | clef |

### Two Separately-Sounded Consonants at the Beginning and Two at the End of a Word

#### Short E

| fleck | cress | clench | blend | press |
|-------|-------|--------|-------|-------|
| smell | snell | thresh | crest | stench |
| spend | bless | sketch | drench | swell |
| French | fresh | tress | trend | trench |
| quest | spent | dress | speck | swept |
| quench | cleft | spell | flesh | dwell |

*Non-Phonic:*  trek

## LESSON 40—(Continued)

### EXERCISES

"Fred, can you spell?" "Why do you ask?" "If you can spell, then spell *flash*." "Which do you mean? We spell *flash* of light with an *a*, and *flesh*, which is meat, with an *e*." Fred has a nose bleed. His nose bled last night. Fred does not sleep well at night. He can't breathe well. He went to sleep at ten and slept till three. A trench is a long, deep ditch. Can you play chess? To play a game of chess, one must use his brains.

At night I clean and press my dress and mend my hose. Eve says, "When I go to sleep, I pray to God to keep us well and bless us." When I sneeze, Dad says, "God bless you!" Fred says: "When I get up, I dress. I put on my pants, clean socks, and shoes. I eat an egg, bran with cream, and toast in my milk. Then I go to class. There I read and spell and take my French. I can't speak French well yet." Meats and fish must be fresh to be fit to eat. You can tell by the smell when fish and meat are not fresh. A thing that is stale is not fresh.

"We press your coat while you wait." We press grapes to make wine. Spend your time well and your time will be well spent. A well bred man says and does the right thing at the right time.

## LESSON 41

**Two Separately-Sounded Consonants at the Beginning of a Word**

**Long I**

| bride | bribe | swine | brine | drive |
| slide | gripe | pride | thrive | slime |
| smile | smite | spine | crime | tribe |
| spite | bright | fright | slight | flight |
| plight | twine | shrine | prize | blithe |

## LESSON 41—(Continued)

### Two Separately-Sounded Consonants at the Beginning of a Word

#### Short I

| 1 | | | 2 | |
|---|---|---|---|---|
| gripe | - | grip | prime | - | prim |
| slime | - | slim | spine | - | spin |
| spite | - | spit | tripe | - | trip |

| | | | | |
|---|---|---|---|---|
| brim | grin | clip | brick | still |
| skiff | grim | switch | Swiss | twitch |
| swim | slit | cliff | click | slip |
| sniff | thrill | skill | crib | stiff |
| skin | trick | stick | flick | drill |
| trim | flip | drip | grill | Smith |
| skip | shrill | twin | twig | stitch |

### Two Separately-Sounded Consonants at the Beginning and Two at the End of a Word

#### Short I

| | | | |
|---|---|---|---|
| blink | stilt | bring | sling |
| brink | frisk | fling | stint |
| grist | crimp | swing | cling |
| crisp | switch | drink | sting |
| brisk | print | clinch | flinch |
| primp | blimp | shrink | shrimp |
| drift | thrift | twist | flint |

## LESSON 41—(Continued)

### EXERCISES

Mr. Smith is a big, fat man. Mrs. Smith is slight and slim, but trim. Trim means neat. The Smiths have one son. His name is Cliff. Cliff is bright. He won the class prize last year and a trip to Spain. "A stitch in time saves nine." Don't sit and grin. Smile while you may. A glass of fresh milk is the best drink. Drink much of it. The sting of a bee is like the prick of a pin. It pains and makes the skin swell up.

Eat your toast while it is still hot and crisp. I can read well if it is in print. It takes skill to spin a top. It is quite a thrill to see Cliff swim. He can swim like a duck and do tricks on his back. Dick fell off a swing and he slit his chin. He has a stiff neck and his hand is still in a sling.

The pen Mr. Flint gave me has a steel clip. "Who will bring me a glass of milk to drink?" "I will," said Slim. "I will," said Cliff. "Let us flip a dime and see who will bring the drink." Swine thrive on bran. To thrive means to get big and fat. We use twine to tie with. Be sure to tie the twine tight. To cling is to stick to a thing. A lock-smith can drill a hole in steel. To drive is to chase. Don't chase the cat. Don't drive fast at night; you may not get there.

## LESSON 42

### Two Separately-Sounded Consonants at the Beginning of a Word

#### Long O

| broke | froze | groan  | throat | smoke  |
| stove | stole | probe  | smote  | clove  |
| spoke | grove | globe  | drove  | throne |
| close | float | clothe | stone  | slope  |
| floe  | throe | croak  | gloat  | fro    |

## LESSON 42—(Continued)

### Two Separately-Sounded Consonants at the Beginning of a Word

#### Short O

| | | | | |
|---|---|---|---|---|
| drop | spot | plot | blot | clot |
| frog | prod | slop | from | prop |
| slot | trot | flop | snob | flog |
| stop | clog | crop | throb | smog |

### Two Consonants at the Beginning and Two at the End of a Word

#### Short O

| | | | | |
|---|---|---|---|---|
| gloss | front | stock | floss | block |
| clock | prong | scoff | blotch | flock |
| frock | throng | crock | Scotch | smock |
| bronze | crotch | frost | blond | cross |
| frond | prompt | cloth | blonde | broth |

*Non-Phonic:* bloc broad gross

## EXERCISES

Do you see that red light? A red light means stop. If you do not stop, you will pay a fine. A grove is a path-way with trees on each side. A crock is a big pot made of clay. Where there is smoke, there must be fire.

Mr. Stone is Scotch. He has a shop a block long. In his shop you can buy pots and pans, clocks and crocks, socks and shoes, globes and clothes. We drove by there last week to see his stock of stoves. We need a coal stove. The grate in my stove broke, and we can't use it as

## LESSON 42—(Continued)

it is. We spoke with Mr. Stone, but he said it is late and they close the shop at six o'clock.

Drop a dime in the slot and you will get a big pack of gum. A slot is the same as a slit, which is a long cut in a thing. A grease stain makes a spot.

"We drove at a trot" means to drive step by step and not too fast. To float is not the same as to swim. When you float, you just drift, but when you swim, you go fast. A lot of sheep is a flock of sheep. We say, "He has a whole flock of geese," and, "Flocks of goats graze near the lake." A frog lives in a pond. The frog does not run; it just hops. To hop is to jump. Stole is the past tense of steal. The tramp stole my clothes while I went to see Mr. Sloan on the next block.

He does not get much gross pay. Flo has to cross a broad road to reach the block where Mr. Frost has his shoe shop. When Mr. Frost has a sale, there is a throng in his shop. The base of the lamp is made of bronze.

## LESSON 43

### Two Separately-Sounded Consonants at the Beginning of a Word

#### Long U and Long Y

| blue | glue | true | flue | prune |
| flute | brute | crude | fruit | plume |
| clue | cruse | prude | bruise | cruise |

| cry | dry | fly | sly | try |
| pry | ply | fry | sky | sty |
|  | style | spy | Clyde |  |

## LESSON 43—(Continued)

### Two Separately-Sounded Consonants at the Beginning of a Word

#### Short U

| | | | | |
|---|---|---|---|---|
| spun | scum | swum | shrub | slush |
| crux | stun | stub | shrug | plum |
| bluff | spud | plus | drum | snub |
| glum | slum | stud | plug | clutch |
| cluck | slug | flush | thrush | fluff |
| scuff | plush | snuff | pluck | crutch |
| crush | truck | blush | stuff | stuck |
| gruff | club | brush | drug | grub |

### Two Separately-Sounded Consonants at the Beginning and Two at the End of a Word

#### Short U and Short Y

| | | | | |
|---|---|---|---|---|
| grunt | stung | slump | swung | shrunk |
| plunk | blunt | trump | brunt | crust |
| thrust | brunch | trust | stump | drunk |
| clung | stunt | spunk | crunch | clump |
| slung | plump | trunk | flung | flunk |
| crypt | | | | tryst |

*Non-Phonic:*  *truth   skunk   skull   skulk*

# LESSON 43—(Continued)

## EXERCISES

My flag is red, white, and blue. It is the flag of the land of the brave and the free. When I get up, I brush my teeth, but I do not bruise my gums. Then I fry my eggs and eat them with toast. One day we have grape-fruit and one day prunes. A prune is a dry plum. I like plum pie when the crust is crisp. We eat brunch at 11:30 a.m. each day.

I brush my shoes and suit and put them on. Then I pack my lunch in a box so that I do not crush the fruit. I put on my blue coat. I like its style. I can't use my black coat as it has shrunk. Mr. Clyde Scott will teach me to play the drum and the flute. Mr. Crump drives a U. S. A. mail truck. One day he got stuck in the mud, and the mud stuck to the wheels like glue.

One who gets drunk can't get a job and can't drive a truck. You can't trust a man who gets drunk. You can't trust a man who bluffs. A bluff is not the truth. You must not trust a spy. A spy is sly. If you have a task to do, don't bluff and don't give up, but try and try and you'll be sure to get it done. Don't say a thing that is not true and you will not have to blush. The men in planes fly sky-high. A fly has wings. They keep swine in a sty. If you limp, use a crutch. A crutch is a stick that helps the lame to stand up. A cruse is a pot. A cruse is a cup, too. To cruise means to sail. The skunk hid in the shack.

# REVIEW

## Short A - Short E

| Column 1 | Column 2 | Column 3 |
|---|---|---|
| and - end | bad - bed | land - lend |
| Dan - den | fad - fed | sand - send |
| lag - leg | pan - pen | last - lest |
| man - men | tan - ten | band - bend |
| sat - set | bat - bet | past - pest |
| ham - hem | mat - met | pant - pent |

## Long E - Short I - Short Y

| Column 1 | Column 2 | Column 3 |
|---|---|---|
| eat - it | heap - hip | bead - bid |
| eel - ill | deem - dim | feel - fill |
| ease - is | seal - sill | heat - hit |
| beat - bit | heed - hid | lead - lid |
| deed - did | seen - sin | seat - sit |
| feet - fit | peel - pill | sleep - slip |
| keen - kin | leap - lip | green - grin |
| meal - mill | heal - hill | steal - still |
| seek - sick | deep - dip | greet - grit |
| read - rid | bean - bin | sleet - slit |
| lean - Lynn | seed - Syd | meat - myth |

## REVIEW—(Continued)

### Short O - Short U

| Column 1 | Column 2 | Column 3 |
| --- | --- | --- |
| cot - cut | hog - hug | shot - shut |
| hot - hut | doll - dull | sock - suck |
| rob - rub | lock - luck | dock - duck |
| not - nut | log - lug | stock - stuck |
| pop - pup | non - nun | crotch - crutch |

### Short E - Short I - Short Y

| Column 1 | Column 2 | Column 3 |
| --- | --- | --- |
| pen - pin | bet - bit | crept - crypt |
| den - din | set - sit | sled - slid |
| Ben - bin | let - lit | check - chick |
| ken - kin | bed - bid | bless - bliss |
| net - nit | tell - till | clench - clinch |
| led - lid | pet - pit | spell - spill |
| red - rid | bell - bill | swell - swill |
| sell - sill | mess - miss | trek - trick |
| fell - fill | ten - tin | clef - cliff |
| met - mitt | hem - him | fleck - flick |

# PART II

## Words of More Than One Syllable

## Suffixes and Prefixes

---

### INTRODUCTION TO LESSON 44

| - - y at the End of a Word |||
|---|---|---|
| - - ay = a | - - y = i | - - ye = i |

| | | | |
|---|---|---|---|
| day | say | by | dye |
| may | hay | shy | rye |
| way | lay | why | lye |

| Suffix —ly | - - y as i in *it* or long e |
|---|---|

| | |
|---|---|
| weekly | dimly |
| nightly | wisely |
| sadly | thickly |

# LESSON 44

## Two-Syllable Words (Suffixed)

| —ly | —ful | —less | —ness |
|---|---|---|---|
| main-ly | pain-ful | aim-less | weak-ness |
| safe-ly | hate-ful | shame-less | mean-ness |
| vainly | faithful | faithless | madness |
| neatly | gainful | seedless | thickness |
| yearly | shameful | fearless | sickness |
| highly | fearful | needless | likeness |
| namely | cheerful | matchless | slyness |
| timely | hopeful | restless | quickness |
| lonely | rightful | helpless | neatness |
| solely | thankful | reckless | shyness |
| purely | bashful | listless | paleness |
| lastly | handful | godless | sameness |
| costly | sinful | jobless | deepness |
| justly | cupful | luckless | dullness |
| plainly | playful | dustless | gladness |
| bravely | fretful | brainless | blackness |
| frankly | skillful | stainless | cleanness |
| gladly | spiteful | speechless | clearness |
| clearly | fruitful | sleeveless | freshness |
| freely | frightful | sleepless | stillness |
| sweetly | trustful | smokeless | brightness |
| blithely | truthful | sightless | vastness |

## LESSON 44—(Continued)

## DRILL

| | | | |
|---|---|---|---|
| blissful | spotless | crudely | rimless |
| flatly | slightly | meatless | closely |
| blameless | tactless | gruffly | grateful |
| gravely | prickly | briskly | highness |
| promptly | useless | wishful | brightly |
| sadness | hatless | stiffness | likely |
| quickly | lifeless | gleeful | sweetness |
| freshly | useful | dryness | grimly |

*Non-Phonic:* daily   wholly   only

## EXERCISES

Dress plainly but neatly. It is needless to spend much on costly clothes. A dress that has no sleeves is a sleeveless dress. You may not have costly clothes, but they can still be spotless and stainless.

We pave the roads to make them mudless and dustless. On a dustless road, we can see clearly and drive safely. Give freely of what you have. Give gladly and be thankful that you can give. When you feel sick, be cheerful and hopeful. Sadness surely will not help you. A sick man may be listless, but need not be hopeless. He is restless and sleepless, and weakness makes him listless and fretful. A skillful man who is well and jobless is not luckless. He is just helpless and aimless. Don't be bashful, seek and ask. Shyness will not get you the job.

Some sickness is painful like the sting of the bee. Some is painless, but is sickness just the same. In the stillness of the night we can think clearly, but in the blackness of the night we can't see clearly.

## LESSON 44—(Continued)

Clyde said, "A godless man is likely to be a sinful man, and one who is spiteful is hateful." Meanness just makes him hateful. One who can read need not feel lonely, and one who can sing sweetly need not be fearful at night. Say what you have to say plainly. Speak clearly. Tell the truth frankly and bravely.

## LESSON 45

### Two-Syllable Words

### Suffix —y

| 1 | 2 | 3 | 4 |
|---|---|---|---|
| { rain-y<br>{ rai-ny | { haz(e̸-y<br>{ ha-zy | sun-ny | hand-y |
|  |  | foggy | windy |
| needy | wavy | funny | rusty |
| leafy | shaky | witty | dusty |
| meaty | shady | puppy | misty |
| leaky | shiny | muddy | silky |
| soapy | bony | chummy | catchy |
| foamy | easy | gummy | sandy |
| brainy | crazy | snappy | cranky |
| creamy | briny | draggy | tricky |
| dreamy | slimy | skinny | crispy |
| sneaky | stony | sloppy | frisky |
| sleepy | smoky | groggy | stocky |
| creepy | rosy | glossy | stuffy |
| fruity | flaky | classy | fluffy |

## LESSON 45—(Continued)

## DRILL

| scanty | fatty | kinky | nasty | rocky |
| crusty | greasy | mighty | holy | husky |
| fleshy | squeaky | creaky | lofty | hefty |
| shabby | slanty | crafty | crunchy | chunky |
| fussy | creepy | baggy | speedy | thrifty |
| tiny | buggy | bulky | sleety | gravy |
| muggy | fishy | lucky | clumsy | navy |

|  - - ie  |  | - - ey |  |
|---|---|---|---|
| prairie | stymie | donkey | galley |
| eerie | pixie | alley | valley |
| caddie | collie | jockey | hockey |
| Dixie | Minnie | volley | trolley |
| Sadie | Susie | cockney | pulley |
| Julie | Maggie | monkey | abbey |

*Non-Phonic:* any many body busy fiery study money honey
*Exceptions:* young magpie

## EXERCISES

Any man who can't do things right is clumsy. Many men, when they get to be sixty just sit, eat, drink, and sleep. A brainy, skillful man does his duty. When it is hot and muggy you feel stuffy. One who is lean is said to be skinny, and one who is fat and fleshy is said to be stocky. You may feel jolly, but don't act silly. To be jolly means to

## LESSON 45—(Continued)

feel happy. Anyone who acts silly has no sense. To be jolly does not cost you a penny, so why not be happy?

I have a collie puppy. His name is Fuzzy. A puppy is a young dog. I made Fuzzy a tiny, cozy home. On sunny days, he is frisky and runs, jumps, and is playful. On chilly, rainy days he is lazy and he just sleeps and sleeps.

We live near a dairy in the valley. In a dairy they sell milk, cream, butter, and cheese and sometimes eggs, too. The lady who lives next to us on the prairie has a baby. The baby has big, blue, dreamy eyes and tiny, chubby hands. The baby can't speak yet, but he can surely cry. A baby must not eat candy. Candy makes him sick and he gets cranky and fretful. He is a busy body. He kicks his feet until he gets weary and sleepy. Then he is put to bed in his crib. A crib is a baby's bed. When it is hot, candy gets sticky like glue.

Mr. Eddie Smith is a man of nearly sixty years, but still handy and cheerful and happy to be helpful. He is big, but skinny and bony, not fleshy. He says while a man lives, he must do his duty gladly and keep busy. On sunny days, you can see him till the land and fix the road. On rainy days, the road is muddy and on windy days, it is dusty. When it is foggy, he can't see well. Then he does things in his home. He roasts the meat and makes crispy toast. He can bake fluffy cakes and fry ducks. He is not sloppy and is not greasy. He does things neatly and cleanly. He likes to study when he has time.

# LESSON 46

## Two-Syllable Words

### Suffix —ing

| 1 | 2 | 3 | 4 |
|---|---|---|---|
| aim-ing | ⎧ bak(e̸-ing | trap-ping | ask-ing |
| raining | ⎩ bak-ing | batting | thanking |
| keeping | saving | begging | resting |
| feeling | biting | letting | helping |
| dealing | rising | digging | singing |
| poaching | hoping | dipping | pinching |
| loading | joking | sobbing | rocking |
| mailing | using | nodding | shocking |
| reading | wiping | budding | hunting |
| waiting | voting | hugging | punching |
| trailing | liking | dragging | drafting |
| claiming | trading | grabbing | standing |
| draining | skating | swimming | smacking |
| paying | blaming | slipping | spending |
| playing | draping | spinning | drinking |
| praying | smiling | stopping | swinging |
| staying | driving | plotting | crushing |
| cleaning | smoking | drumming | plucking |
| bleeding | closing | spitting | trucking |
| floating | craving | skipping | printing |
| training | flaming | dripping | brushing |
| sleeping | blazing | thrilling | stamping |
| dreaming | gluing | spilling | slanting |

## LESSON 46—(Continued)

## DRILL

| trading | slashing | stemming | freezing |
| stocking | twisting | riding | squeezing |
| hopping | stabbing | ridding | stepping |
| aiding | grating | suing | sniffing |
| adding | flipping | poaching | pressing |
| acting | stunning | filing | camping |
| itching | sketching | filling | blushing |
| ending | etching | taking | slaving |
| stitching | sloping | tacking | clapping |
| squealing | steaming | stacking | sticking |
| clinging | whipping | quizzing | sneezing |

### Adding Suffix -ing to Words Ending in -ie

| lie - lying | hie - hying |
| tie - tying | die - dying |
| vie - vying | (dye - dyeing) |

## EXERCISES

We can add gladness and meaning to life by doing something useful and by trying to reach a high goal. When we have a job to do, there must be no stopping, no slipping, and no loafing.

Let's see what some of us are doing. Jimmy is flying a plane. He says it is thrilling to go up in a plane. Henry is loading trains, trucks, and ships at the dock. Susie is in training to wait on the sick, and Jenny is dressing the bleeding and ailing. Sally is aiding those who are needy, and Tillie is filing, typing, and mailing. Sadie is teaching, Johnny is preaching, and Danny is mining coal. Bobby and Andy are

## LESSON 46—(Continued)

vying for the prize in sketching. Sydney and Lillie are selling clothing in a shop.

Mr. Flamming is planting, tilling, and hoeing in the blazing sun, trying to raise a big crop. His wife is milking, cleaning, sweeping, and mending. They have five sons. Three are in the navy, one is acting in a play in the valley, and one is helping Mr. and Mrs. Flamming at home.

In the evening, Mr. Flamming spends his time resting, reading, and smoking his pipe. Just when he is dozing off, someone yells, "Hi, Jimmy, it's time to go shopping. Benning's is having a sale this week, and the cost of buying seeds and plants is cheap." It is Mr. Eddie Flushing. It is raining, and he is dripping wet. His clothing is sticking to his skin. Mr. Flamming says, "Oh, let's skip it tonight. There is no use going in the drenching rain." "Well, then," Mr. Flushing says, "why am I standing here spending my time doing nothing, when I have many tasks to do at home! We must use the time on hand wisely. I'll be seeing you in a day or so. Bye, bye!"

## LESSON 47

Suffix —ed, Meaning Past Time

e silent

| 1 | 2 | 3 |
|---|---|---|
| { aim-ed<br>{ aimed | { name-d<br>{ named | { can-ned<br>{ canned |
| mailed | saved | gagged |
| nailed | gazed | begged |
| rained | lined | dimmed |
| sealed | timed | chilled |
| seemed | shined | robbed |
| feared | hoed | rubbed |

## LESSON 47—(Continued)

| 1 | 2 | 3 |
|---|---|---|
| cheered | dozed | hugged |
| wheeled | used | chummed |
| gained | sued | pinned |
| chained | cured | sinned |
| healed | shaved | grabbed |
| drained | braved | dragged |
| trailed | flamed | trimmed |
| cleaned | craved | clogged |
| steamed | bribed | skinned |
| smeared | smiled | throbbed |
| cruised | closed | spanned |
| groaned | bathed | spelled |
| trained | glazed | stemmed |
| roamed | grazed | shunned |

**Suffix -ed, -e silent, d with the sound of t, after:**

| x - f | s - sh | ch - p | k - ck |
|---|---|---|---|
| taxed | chased | bleached | baked |
| mixed | passed | fetched | backed |
| fixed | blessed | clinched | leaked |
| coaxed | missed | clutched | licked |
| boxed | crossed | wiped | liked |
| sniffed | smashed | whipped | soaked |
| scoffed | threshed | slumped | socked |
| puffed | wished | reached | plucked |
| stuffed | crushed | helped | stoked |
| bluffed | brushed | hopped | stocked |
| waxed | kissed | hoped | smacked |
| vexed | mashed | stamped | blinked |
| scuffed | creased | patched | smoked |
| jinxed | sloshed | duped | risked |

# LESSON 47—(Continued)

## EXERCISES

Mrs. Bailey baked shad for the evening meal. Tom, the young cat, who had been lying near the stove, smelled the fish and begged for some. When Mrs. Bailey filled his dish, Tom sniffed at the shad and then quickly ate it. He did not have to be coaxed. Tom licked Mrs. Bailey's hand as a thank you.

Van teased Rusty and then chased him. On the way, Van slipped and fell into the lake and got drenched. He stumped his toe and bruised his leg, too. This cured Van from chasing Rusty. When Van reached the bank of the lake, he dried his wet body with the bleached cloth.

The fire spanned five miles and blazed and roared. It smoked up many homes. The wind whipped the fire up to the bluff. Felled trees blocked the roads for miles, and thick smoke dimmed the bright, sunny sky. Trained men braved the fiery roads and saved many homes. Breathing the smoke made some of the men sick. When it rained, the men cheered, as the rain helped to quench the flames. When the fire had been stopped, the men quickly cleared the clogged roads.

We are blessed with many things. We don't have much, but we are still lucky.

Mrs. Sweeney plucked, cleaned, and soaked the hen. Then she drained, stuffed, and baked it. Ms. Denny trimmed the hem of my dress and then pinned and stitched it.

# LESSON 48

### Suffix —ed
### e of -ed sounded after d and t

| 1 | 2 | 3 | 4 |
|---|---|---|---|
| { aid-ed<br>aided | { hate-d<br>hated | { pat-ted<br>patted | { hand-ed<br>handed |
| heated | rated | padded | lasted |
| needed | faded | wedded | tended |
| roasted | voted | fitted | rested |
| cheated | noted | nodded | lifted |
| waited | quoted | rotted | landed |
| seated | shaded | budded | mended |
| braided | traded | fretted | planted |
| pleaded | stated | blotted | branded |
| greeted | graded | plodded | printed |
| bloated | prided | skidded | trusted |
| loaded | slated | studded | twisted |
| coated | glided | spotted | drifted |
| floated | plated | plotted | frosted |

## DRILL

| | | | |
|---|---|---|---|
| blazed | sneaked | stitched | trotted |
| grated | treated | blinked | swelled |
| spaded | breathed | stinted | pressed |
| dragged | blended | slighted | shredded |
| clasped | drenched | prized | drugged |

## LESSON 48—(Continued)

| drafted | quenched | flocked | bruised |
| slanted | smiled | closed | suited |
| cleaned | drilled | stopped | stumped |
| pleated | flipped | groaned | baited |

## EXERCISES

A penny saved is a penny made. Stanley aimed high and reached his goal. He aided the sick and helped the needy. Edy passed a red light. She'll be fined. We have a puppy. We named it Laddy. We keep him chained sometimes. Laddy used to run away.

We painted the gate red. We tacked a note on it saying, "Wet Paint." My white puppy can't read. He leaned against the gate and rubbed off the paint, so we named him "Red Tail."

Mr. Chase and I went fishing last week. I waited while he shaved and shined his shoes. Mrs. Chase fixed a lunch. She packed it in a box. She added some mixed cakes and roasted peanuts and handed it to him. We rented a boat and sailed away.

At midday we landed at the beach and rested on the sand awhile. We mended the net. It needed it badly. We reached home late, but loaded with fish. We feasted on them a whole week.

We drilled till five and dined at six. I can read it if it is printed clearly and not blotted. We traded with them. They may be trusted. We floated on a raft six days. I brushed my suit and shined my shoes. She had on a pleated dress trimmed in white. He plucked a rose and gave it to me. When I passed by, I greeted them. We had glazed dates with stuffed nuts. What does dated mean? When the day of the month is stamped on a thing, we say it is dated.

My wheels skidded on the sleety road, and we bumped into a tree stump. I skinned my legs and bruised my hands. I plodded up a graded hill. I spotted an inn. There a lady treated my cuts.

# LESSON 49

## Suffixes —s and —es

**—es forms a syllable after a hissing sound:**

| s | sh | x | z | ch |
|---|---|---|---|---|
| dress | wish | tax | buzz | teach |
| dress**es** | wish**es** | tax**es** | buzz**es** | teach**es** |

| 1 | 2 | 3 | 4 |
|---|---|---|---|
| fail-s | shave-s | chase-s | pass-es |
| meets | shines | leases | buzzes |
| soaks | smokes | rises | fixes |
| claims | rules | poses | wishes |
| speaks | gropes | uses | teaches |
| boasts | glides | gazes | catches |
| stands | braves | dozes | razzes |
| helps | spites | sneezes | mixes |
| clings | stakes | grazes | coaxes |
| throbs | wipes | blazes | crushes |
| | | | |
| snail-s | grape-s | base-s | branch-es |
| bails | brides | breezes | blotches |
| teams | clothes | creases | slashes |
| roads | stones | greases | flashes |
| steps | prunes | cruses | boxes |
| stumps | spikes | roses | taxes |
| stilts | scales | cases | dresses |
| blocks | swipes | prizes | crosses |
| clumps | planes | fuses | quizzes |
| scabs | crates | sizes | bunches |

## LESSON 49—(Continued)

### DRILL

| ashes | razes | spires | tests | lisps |
| fixes | lists | ditches | sixes | spades |
| asks | matches | disks | snakes | mashes |
| raises | risks | blesses | tusks | preaches |
| skates | freezes | casts | jests | coaches |
| clashes | masks | boasts | crutches | crusts |
| slides | glimpses | feasts | grasps | sketches |
| squeezes | twists | trusts | flushes | slopes |
| flasks | presses | vexes | shucks | clasps |
| hitches | axes | rasps | crunches | stoves |

### EXERCISES

Amos is a handy man. Mrs. Nelson hired him to do odd things. He rises at six, fixes the fire, and tends to the ashes. He puts the ashes in cans and boxes. He feeds the mules, the pigs, the hens, the ducks, and the geese. He helps with the dishes and shines shoes. He brushes the coats, suits, and dresses, and he cuts branches off the trees and bushes.

Amos has a buddy named Tony. Amos and Tony get along fine. Tony is nicknamed Fatty and Amos is nicknamed Texas. Texas chases Fatty, but he can't run fast, so Texas teases him and Fatty gets mad and fusses. When it is hot, Fatty gets tired quickly. He sits in the shade and dozes. Texas yells at him, "Hey, Lazy Bones, the sun is shining in your eyes." "That's why I keep 'em shut," he yells back.

This is Spears' shop. They sell spades and axes, paints and brushes, skates and greases, nails, spikes, and rakes. Mr. Spears closes at six and comes in when he pleases. We traded with him many years.

## LESSON 49—(Continued)

Mrs. Spears tends the roses. She plucked three bunches of roses and sent them to Miss Neals who teaches on the next block. Miss Neals put the roses in vases and set them on the desk.

## LESSON 50

> Two-Syllable Words
>
> Suffix —er Meaning "More"
>
> (Comparative Degree Adjectives or Adverbs)
>
> (Suffix —er is used when comparing two persons, places, or things.)

| 1 | 2 | 3 | 4 |
|---|---|---|---|
| deep-er | fine-r | big-ger | fast-er |
| keener | later | fatter | richer |
| dearer | paler | redder | thicker |
| nearer | safer | thinner | lighter |
| weaker | wiser | hotter | quicker |
| sweeter | whiter | sadder | blacker |
| cleaner | purer | wetter | fresher |
| plainer | wider | dimmer | brighter |
| dryer | closer | gladder | slighter |
| steeper | braver | flatter | crisper |

# LESSON 50—(Continued)

### Suffix —er Meaning the Person Who or the Thing Which Does Whatever the Root Word Indicates

### (Nouns)

| 1 | 2 | 3 | 4 |
|---|---|---|---|
| wait-er | bake-r | tan-ner | sing-er |
| keeper | diver | robber | rocker |
| teacher | voter | chopper | fisher |
| trainer | trader | trapper | cracker |
| trailer | skater | swimmer | slacker |
| preacher | driver | stopper | printer |
| sleeper | glazer | drummer | planter |
| waiver | bather | blotter | drifter |
| cruiser | tuner | shutter | mender |

### —er Not Suffixed

| | | | |
|---|---|---|---|
| mother | summer | slumber | coffer |
| wonder | letter | butter | rubber |
| stutter | better | zipper | winter |
| other | bother | suffer | mutter |
| blunder | plunder | simmer | number |
| brother | sister | lumber | under |
| thunder | trigger | timber | supper |
| fodder | kipper | refer | somber |
| dither | dinner | gather | shudder |
| banner | smother | amber | member |

## LESSON 50—(Continued)

| finger | confer | rather | litter |
| blazer | temper | bitter | tamper |
| pepper | offer  | wicker | whether |
| wither | spider | slither | after |

## EXERCISES

July is hotter than June. This cake is much fresher and sweeter than the one we had last week. Do your duty. Don't be a slacker. This cracker is crisper than the rest. Put litter in the trash can.

A steamer is a ship that runs by steam. One who drives fast is a speeder. The glazer fixes the glass in the frame. A trapper is a hunter, and a trader is a dealer. A stopper is used to stop a leak. The drummer is beating the drum with sticks. The other meaning of drummer is salesman, so we can say a drummer is one who drums up trade.

Polly said, "A preacher is a godly man who teaches the right way of living." The rocker is made of fine lumber. After dinner last night, I mailed the letter to my brother Willie who lives in Texas. He has been teaching in the upper grades for a long time. His wife's mother and sister are teachers of reading, spelling, and math.

I said, "I have two sisters and just one brother." My sister said, "I have two brothers and just one sister." Is the speaker a sister or a brother?

# LESSON 51

### Two-Syllable Words

### Suffix —est Meaning "Most"

### (Superlative Degree Adjectives or Adverbs)

### (Suffix —est is used when comparing three or more persons, places, or things.)

| 1 | 2 | 3 | 4 |
|---|---|---|---|
| gay-est | safe-st | sad-dest | fast-est |
| neatest | palest | fattest | richest |
| keenest | latest | biggest | thickest |
| dearest | finest | reddest | highest |
| cheapest | ripest | wettest | lightest |
| nearest | whitest | hottest | tightest |
| quaintest | vilest | thinnest | sickest |
| frailest | gravest | gladdest | grandest |
| plainest | closest | flattest | blackest |
| cleanest | crudest | slimmest | freshest |
| sweetest | wisest | dimmest | crispest |

### —ish (means like, belonging to, or of the nature of)

| | | | |
|---|---|---|---|
| self-ish | ticklish | peevish | sickish |
| reddish | Irish | Polish | hoggish |
| sheepish | whitish | pinkish | mannish |
| grayish | sluggish | stylish | Swedish |
| sweetish | modish | impish | greenish |

# LESSON 51—(Continued)

## EXERCISES

In things to eat, get the best, not the biggest and cheapest. The cheapest may be the dearest in the end. Get the freshest meats, butter, eggs, and milk.

In my class, June is the thinnest and Lester is the fattest. Ann is the keenest and the neatest. Jean Manning is the gayest and the richest. In running, Jimmy is the fastest.

My closest kin is my mother. Closest means the same as nearest. Every mother's son is the sweetest and dearest. When things seem blackest, don't give up hope. Of the three sisters, Blanch is younger than Fanny, and I am the youngest. Fanny is frail, Blanch is frailer, and I am the frailest. Mr. Boxer is Irish. He speaks English, Spanish, Swedish, Danish and Polish.

A useless thing is rubbish. Get rid of rubbish. Don't save it. Don't be hoggish and don't be selfish. It is ugly to be hoggish and selfish. One thinking only of himself is hoggish. One who likes to take but dislikes to give is selfish.

The baby is peevish today. She is sickly and restless. Nellie has stylish clothing. Modish has the same meaning as stylish.

# LESSON 52

### Two-Syllable Words
### (Also, in Column 1, Prefix a—)

| 1 | 2 | 3 | 4 | 5 |
|---|---|---|---|---|
| a-wait | at-tain | pa-gan | ad-mire | tab-let |
| asleep | appeal | apex | advise | yonder |
| awake | annex | omit | esteem | crystal |
| alive | assume | iris | entire | tranquil |
| aside | attack | human | endure | system |
| afire | attach | pupil | ignite | fungus |
| amuse | effect | silent | impose | suspend |
| afloat | essay | vinyl | inside | velvet |
| adrift | immune | zenith | invite | neglect |
| arise | inning | quota | indeed | bandit |
| awhile | offend | tyrant | index | hatchet |
| amass | utter | tulip | oblong | stigma |

## DRILL

| | | | | |
|---|---|---|---|---|
| insect | oboe | vessel | alone | tyro |
| sudden | tennis | crisis | conduct | queasy |
| climax | connect | padlock | stipend | addict |
| daisy | raisin | enlist | mammoth | raven |
| away | inject | gossip | freedom | oppose |
| soda | fossil | adjust | assist | beside |
| proxy | along | latex | reason | atop |
| abrupt | collect | season | bonnet | admit |
| collapse | rotate | commute | again | Sunday |
| among | shatter | ago | suffix | Monday |

# LESSON 52—(Continued)

> "ICK" RULE
> - - ick = one-syllable words
> - - ic = more-than-one-syllable words

| Read Across | | | Drill | |
|---|---|---|---|---|
| brick | - | fabric | music | traffic |
| lick | - | public | attic | cubic |
| nick | - | picnic | plastic | antic |
| pick | - | aspic | skeptic | lactic |
| sick | - | basic | mystic | toxic |
| stick | - | drastic | styptic | pelvic |
| tick | - | frantic | rustic | tunic |

> The spelling of the "K" sound is determined in each syllable individually. Refer to Lessons 19 and 25 for the rules.

| Read Across | | | Read Across | | |
|---|---|---|---|---|---|
| to-ken | - | token | va-cate | - | vacate |
| vi-king | - | viking | bea-con | - | beacon |
| whis-ky | - | whisky | lo-cust | - | locust |
| blan-ket | - | blanket | a-cross | - | across |
| nap-kin | - | napkin | trun-cate | - | truncate |
| pes-ky | - | pesky | con-clude | - | conclude |
| a-kin | - | akin | mas-cot | - | mascot |
| ink-ling | - | inkling | dis-cuss | - | discuss |

## LESSON 52—(Continued)

### Read Across

| | | |
|---|---|---|
| in-crease | - | increase |
| ac-cuse | - | accuse |
| stuc-co | - | stucco |
| oc-cult | - | occult |
| ac-crue | - | accrue |
| ac-claim | - | acclaim |
| ac-quaint | - | acquaint |
| lac-tate | - | lactate |

### Read Across

| For Spelling | | For Syllables | | Whole Root Word |
|---|---|---|---|---|
| roc-ket | - | rock-et | - | rocket |
| brac-kish | - | brack-ish | - | brackish |
| tac-ky | - | tack-y | - | tacky |

*Non-Phonic:* biscuit  reckon  beckon  jackal

## EXERCISES

### On A Picnic

Next Sunday there will be a picnic on Long Beach. I have tickets. I think I'll invite Jane Quinn and Jack Wilson to go with us. There is Jack. I beckon to him. I ask him if he'd like to come along on a picnic. He says, "Yes, indeed." He asks me where and when it will be. I tell him. I give him a ticket. He reads: "Picnic,

# LESSON 52—(Continued)

Long Beach, Sunday, June tenth. Music by Milton's big band. Admit one." He puts the ticket in his pocket.

Then I went to see Jane. Mrs. Quinn tells me that Jane is not at home. She went away sometime ago to take a music lesson. She will play a solo next Friday. I say that the reason I came is to invite Jane to go on a picnic. "Thanks a lot," Mrs. Quinn says, "but I can't let Jane go alone." "I shall abide by your wishes. Then why don't you come along with us?" I asked. "I assure you that you will be amused, and you can advise us youngsters in the conduct of some of the games."

It is Sunday, June tenth, five a.m. I am wide awake. I ran up to the attic to get my tennis racket and a basket. I put a roast chicken, a packet of bacon, ham biscuits, a box of crackers, some napkins, a cheese pie, coffee, and some fruit inside the basket. We got to the bus just in time. "May I assist you into the bus, Mrs. Quinn?" Jane sat beside me, and Mrs. Quinn sat beside Mr. Quinn in the next seat. The bus left at six. We planned to reach Long Beach by nine. We had a cheerful time.

A bucket is a pail. A kitten is a young cat. A chicken is a young hen. Wicked means sinful and sinful is evil. A ticket is a pass. A bandit is a wicked man. Absent means "not here." A basket is made of reeds. Alike means "the same." Abed is to be in bed, and atop is to be on top. Monday comes after Sunday. Clothing made of fabric in which nylon and cotton are combined is supposed to last for a long time.

In the last game of the season, which will be played between the Yankees and the White Sox, there will be a contest for the pennant. The athletes on the winning team will split the other prizes among themselves. The Yankees' mascot is a frisky kitten named Trinket.

# LESSON 53

## Two-Syllable Words (Prefixed)

| 1 ex— | 2 un— | 3 re— | 4 de— |
|---|---|---|---|
| exhale | unfit | repeat | detest |
| extract | undue | refill | detain |
| expand | untie | regain | detract |
| exile | unwell | reload | defeat |
| expire | unwise | relapse | define |
| expose | unjust | revive | debate |
| extend | unchain | reprint | depress |
| expel | unlike | retire | defend |
| expense | unload | remake | deduct |
| excuse | unlock | rename | delay |
| extinct | unsafe | refine | detect |
| expend | unpack | repay | degree |
| exit | unlatch | relax | devise |
| extrude | untrue | refit | depose |

## DRILL

| | | | | |
|---|---|---|---|---|
| detail | explain | refresh | until | nonstop |
| explode | reveal | undo | resume | respect |
| request | exist | reject | express | dismiss |
| display | undress | decline | inquire | extra |
| retreat | impure | require | refuse | react |
| unclean | retail | insane | influx | unbend |

109

## LESSON 53—(Continued)

| revolve | disclose | release | under | include |
| inflict | refrain | dispense | result | resist |
| reside | extreme | restock | expect | induct |
| incline | recline | exact | desire | retell |
| retake | unless | repeal | inhale | insult |

## EXERCISES

In case of fire, go to the nearest exit and leave quickly, but do not run. The red light nearest to you is where the nearest exit is. The safest thing to do is to take a seat nearest the exit. Use the fire escape. To escape is to get away safely.

At camp we rise at six and retire at nine. At dusk we must be inside the camp gate. At sunset we lock the gate and unlock it again at sunrise. It is unwise and unsafe to go alone late at night.

Among the pupils, Edwin is the best. We admire and esteem him highly. To be exact, he is A-one in conduct. He attends to his tasks and does not delay. He will not refuse a request to assist at any time. You don't have to repeat your request. He will do it when you ask, unless he is unwell. Even then he will not relax. He does not neglect a thing and will not stop until it is done, as nothing will detain him. Unlike the rest of us, he detests gossip, and he seeks to defeat one who is unjust. It is a delight to hear him debate. His desire is to be right and not merely to win. He defends his rights and respects the rights of the other man.

Exact is "just right." Delay is "to put off." Delay means to say, "I'll do it later." To request is to ask and to assist is to help. Repeat means "say it again." Unwell is the same as sick. To detest is to dislike. A gossip is a tell-tale.

# LESSON 54

## U

| | | | |
|---|---|---|---|
| bull | full | pull | put |
| push | bush | pudding | pullet |
| pulpit | bushel | bully | butcher |
| fully | bushy | pushed | putting |
| pulled | pushing | bushes | pushes |
| bullet | bullish | pulley | bullfrog |

## V

### Long vowel before v

| | | | |
|---|---|---|---|
| shave | lever | even | cleaver |
| hive | fever | oval | rival |
| clove | diver | evil | revere |
| drive | event | lively | over |
| wave | quaver | driver | clover |

### Short vowel before v

| | | | | |
|---|---|---|---|---|
| have | level | sever | living | bevel |
| give | given | above | ever | vivid |
| love | driven | seven | giving | shovel |
| shove | clever | every | river | gavel |
| | sliver | liver | shiver | rivet |
| | quiver | never | novel | divine |

### Vowel before v both long and short

live          dove

## LESSON 54—(Continued)

## EXERCISES

"Did you ever see a bull fight?" "No, I don't think I'd like to see one." A bull fight is not a bull fighting a bull, but a man fighting a bull. A pullet is a young hen.

The hunter puts a bullet in his gun. He aims and then he fires. The butcher sells meats. The meat of a young bull is the best beef. My mother can make the best puddings. Last Sunday my mother made a pudding full of raisins.

This is a rose bush. We have many rose bushes. Not every bush is a rose bush. We will put up a pulley line. I hung my clothes on the pulley line today. It is easy to push and pull the pulley line even when it is full.

Seven is the number after six. On the seventh day we rest. One and six makes seven. We have seven days in a week. "Every dog has his day." We had a very lovely Easter. Every summer we live near the river. We bathe in the river every day. It is lovely there in the summer. There is never a dull day. "Did you ever bathe in a river in the winter?" "No, not I. I get the shivers even to think of it." To shiver means to shake. Shiver is the same as quiver.

Every living thing has a right to live and be happy. Never put off a task you have to do today. One meaning of level is even. We say "a level cupful." But even has meanings other than level. The severe winter is having a bad effect upon the highways in this state.

# LESSON 55

| Three Consonants at the Beginning of a Word | | | | |
|---|---|---|---|---|
| scr- | spl- | spr- | str- | squ- |

| | | | |
|---|---|---|---|
| scrape | splash | strain | street |
| scrap | split | strand | stream |
| scratch | splint | strap | streak |
| screech | spray | strike | stress |
| scream | sprain | strife | stretch |
| screen | sprang | stride | strove |
| scribe | spree | strive | stroke |
| script | spring | stripe | strong |
| scrimp | sprung | string | struck |
| scrub | spry | strip | strung |
| squeal | squeeze | squeak | straight |
| strict | squire | squint | sprint |
| strength | strode | strut | spleen |

## DRILL

| | | | |
|---|---|---|---|
| scraped | scrapped | stretches | stretched |
| scrubs | scrubbing | stripped | straighten |
| splinter | straps | strictly | striped |
| squeezes | sprightly | scrimping | scrubbed |
| stretcher | splitting | splashed | splashes |
| splendid | stranded | spraying | sprained |
| striking | strikers | strapped | streamlined |
| stresses | sprocket | squeamish | strengthen |

113

## LESSON 55—(Continued)

### Three Consonants at the End of a Word

| | | |
|---|---|---|
| glimpse | attempt | against |
| midst | length | prompt |
| tempt | exempt | dreamt |

### EXERCISES

We live on this street. What street is this? This is Spring Street. Spring is a season of the year. A spring is a well. A river is a stream, and a streamer is a long flag. The U. S. A. flag has seven red stripes and six white stripes. A strip of land is a long, straight stretch of land. Straight means running in an even, straight line. If your shoe is tight and pinches you, the shoemaker can stretch it but slightly. Much stretching will split the shoe wide open. Rubber can be stretched better than anything else.

Yes, I have seen when that big brute sprang upon that frail man and struck him with a thick strap. The strong have no right to strike the weak. It is a crime, and it is cruel. To spring is to jump, and sprang means "jumped." A strap is a belt. To strike is to beat and struck means "did beat." To squeeze is to press. We crush fruit by squeezing it. After we have eaten, we gather the scraps and give them to the cat and dog. One who buys junk is said to be a scrap dealer.

My bed is made of steel. It has three slats. On the slats is a spring and on the spring, the mattress. I have a splinter in my finger. I'll ask the druggist to please extract the splinter.

Mrs. Flint is a very thrifty lady. She mends and scrubs, cleans and bakes, scrimps and saves, trying to make ends meet. Mrs. Flint's husband makes big strides to reach his goal. He is striving to buy a home. He strove his whole life, putting penny to penny.

## LESSON 55—(Continued)

I think a leak has sprung in my rear tire. I better see and make sure. They say, "A stitch in time saves nine." My wheels squeak. They need greasing. To scream is the same as to screech. It means a shrill cry. The man who screamed "Help, help!" must have been struck and in much pain.

## LESSON 56

al

| 1 | 2 | 3 |
|---|---|---|
| ail - Al - all | tale - tall | wail - wall - waltz |
| gale - gal - gall | mail - mall | bale - ball - bald |
| pail - pal - pall | stale - stall | fail - fall - false |

4

hail - Hal - hall - halt

### DRILL

| | | | | |
|---|---|---|---|---|
| all | ball | called | fallen | galling |
| hall | call | calling | stalled | altered |
| tall | salt | salty | stalling | smaller |
| wall | false | scalded | installed | smallest |
| bald | small | falsely | also | taller |
| halt | stall | malted | falling | tallest |
| malt | calls | halted | always | recalled |

*Non-Phonic: shall  scalp  valve  talc*

# LESSON 56—(Continued)

## EXERCISES

In the spring and summer we play baseball. In the fall and winter we play basketball. A baseball is smaller than a basketball. The one who strikes the baseball is called the "batter." We have a small kitchen. A clock hangs on the kitchen wall. Near the gas stove, there is the pantry. In the pantry we keep all the dishes and the pots and pans, also the salt and pepper shakers, matches, and soda crackers. Between the steps leading up from the basement and the kitchen, there is a small hall.

Mother called up the butcher to bring us a chicken. Mother opened the chicken. Right by the liver is a small green sack which contains a bitter liquid called gall. Mother cleaned the chicken, then she scalded it and put it in the small roaster. She salted and seasoned it, and then she put the roaster into the hot oven.

Mr. Hall is a tall man. He is bald. His son Walter is one inch taller than he is, and his youngest son is the tallest of the three. As I recall, Walter has always been the best batter on his ball team. We used to call him "Long Legged Walt." He always made a home run.

"All is well that ends well."

# LESSON 57

## Long A Before R
Spelled **air** as in ch**air** or **are** as in sc**are**

| Read Across | | | Read Across | | |
|---|---|---|---|---|---|
| 1 | 2 | 3 | 1 | 2 | 3 |
| aim | am | air | cane | can | care |
| faith | fat | fair | rate | rat | rare |
| paid | pad | pair | bake | back | bare |

## DRILL

| | | | | |
|---|---|---|---|---|
| air | care | bare | mare | unfair |
| fair | fare | ware | rare | paired |
| hair | hare | dare | blare | upstairs |
| pair | pare | spared | glare | rarest |
| chair | share | flare | scare | rarer |
| stair | stare | snare | square | glaring |
| airy | careful | careless | fairly | squarely |
| fairness | hairy | hairless | staring | squared |
| sharing | barely | daring | sparing | despair |
| rarely | scared | chairs | wares | declared |
| affair | aware | fairest | repair | compare |
| beware | ensnare | parent | farewell | scary |

*Non-Phonic:*  are

117

# LESSON 57—(Continued)

## EXERCISES

To live we must have air, but we can't live on air alone. There is a big affair at Times Square tonight. I rarely go to any affair, but tonight we are all going to hear Dr. Squire speak on "Sharing God's Blessings."

Many things go in pairs as a pair of shoes or a pair of stockings. To pare means to cut away. We pare fruit. We call one who has no hair bald. We have three plush chairs and six plain chairs. The legs of one chair are broken. We will have to repair them.

Stairs is a flight of steps. To stare is to gaze with eyes wide open. I am afraid something is the matter with my son. I call to him to come upstairs, and he just stands still and stares at me. I haven't the strength to run up three flights of stairs so many times.

Be careful with the glassware. Be careful when you cross the street. There are many drivers who are careless. One such driver barely missed hitting me. It is better to be careful than scared. To scare is to frighten.

If you put a lighted match to paper, it will flare up. Flare is a sudden blaze. A spare tire is an extra tire; one not in use. You are hungry, my dear man. Here, take this money and buy yourself a square meal. This is all the cash I can spare.

# LESSON 58

### Short A Before R

**ar** sounded as **r**

| Read Across 1 | | | Read Across 2 | |
|---|---|---|---|---|
| fair | - | far | bare | - bar |
| pair | - | par | mare | - mar |
| chair | - | char | care | - car |
| stair | - | star | scare | - scar |

### Five Sounds of A

#### Read Down

| | | | |
|---|---|---|---|
| bake | faith | cane | pain |
| back | fat | can | pan |
| bare | fair | care | pare |
| bar | far | car | par |
| ball | fall | call | pall |

## DRILL

| | | | |
|---|---|---|---|
| bar | park | carp | march |
| far | bark | dart | chart |
| car | mark | tart | star |
| jar | harmed | darn | scarred |
| tar | farming | carve | started |
| arm | party | sharply | scarves |

119

## LESSON 58—(Continued)

| art    | barn    | shark    | smart    |
| lard   | cart    | marshy   | spark    |
| card   | yard    | harsh    | starve   |
| hard   | dark    | char     | starchy  |
| arch   | ark     | barred   | jarring  |
| arches | armful  | armless  | hardly   |
| tarred | arched  | parked   | darkness |
| partly | parted  | harmful  | harmless |
| afar   | ajar    | apart    | smartest |
| target | varnish | pardon   | carbon   |
| cargo  | farther | hardened | Armand   |

*Non-Phonic:* arc  father

## EXERCISES

This is a public park. In a park, there are many shade trees. A small card is tacked on the bark of each tree. The cards read: "Elm Tree," "Pine Tree," "Oak Tree," "Keep off the Grass," and "Do Not Harm Plants and Trees," which means do not carve your name on the bark of the trees.

After dark, on very hot days, we go to the park to get fresh air and rest. If the park is far, we go by private car or bus. The bus fare is not much. We can reach there by taxi also. One part of the park is called the "Ball Park." They play baseball and tennis there. Those who come in private cars to see the games, park their cars near the bleachers.

Mr. Carp is a farmer. He has a truck farm and chicken farm. On the farm there are barns and barnyards. The barns are covered with tarred paper. He keeps his cars and pushcarts in the barn. A pushcart is a two-wheeled car. In the barnyard there are chickens, ducks, and geese. The pig stalls are barred off, so the swine can't run away.

## LESSON 58—(Continued)

Mr. and Mrs. Carp are a happy pair. Mrs. Carp says that life on a farm is very hard, but if you are willing, you will never have to starve. You will always have plenty to eat. She is right.

A farmer must get up at sunrise when his day starts. His day ends when the stars appear in the sky. Not all the land can be tilled. The land is partly marshy. The winters on the farm are long and dreary. They last to the end of March.

But Mrs. Carp has plenty to do. She gathers the eggs, renders the lard and chicken fat, and skims the cream off the milk. In the evening she darns the hose and makes scarves. Mr. Carp attends to the livestock on the yard. His son Armand spades and hoes the garden.

With his sharp ax, Mr. Carp chops off a tree and splits it into logs. He takes in an armful and puts some on the fire. His arms are scarred, but he is happy and smiles. Only rarely do they go to an affair. When there is a party at a nearby farm, they go to it.

## LESSON 59

| arr | ara | are | ari | aro | aru | ary |
|---|---|---|---|---|---|---|
| narrate | parade | caret | arid | parole | arum | larynx |

(Before the end of the root word)

(Sound of "a" in "ask" or "at" and schwa sound)

| | | | |
|---|---|---|---|
| carry | arrive | parrot | caravan |
| marry | barrel | Carolyn | harass |
| arrest | embarrass | paradise | caress |
| barren | barracks | paralyze | aroma |
| garret | Larry | paradox | parish |
| Barry | arrears | parasite | carat |

## LESSON 59—(Continued)

| Harry   | array    | paraffin | tariff   |
|---------|----------|----------|----------|
| tarry   | carrot   | caraway  | baron    |
| apparel | marinate | sarong   | clarinet |
| carrel  | scarab   | paragon  | charity  |

### EXERCISES

Harry and Larry are twin brothers. You can hardly tell them apart. Harry and Larry will marry the Cary sisters. Harry has a scar over his right eye. It is by that mark that I can tell which is which. They are tall, dark, and handsome. The Cary sisters are fair, have bright blue eyes, and light hair.

Mr. Barry, the farmer, raises carrots. He has to carry the carrots to market to sell them. He ties six or seven carrots together in a bunch, and we buy them in bunches. As a rule, we don't eat the green part, called carrot tops, but they are tasty when prepared right. Larry goes to the market to buy carrots. His mother tells him not to tarry, but to come back quickly. To tarry means to stay away long. "Don't tarry" is the same as "Don't delay."

To narrate is to tell. Mr. Cary will narrate a fairy tale to you. Who can narrate the tale of Jonah in the whale? No one sleeps in the garret. We keep only trunks and barrels in the garret. Some man who can't pay rent will be glad to sleep in the garret.

If we leave at three and if we don't tarry on the way, but drive straight, I think we will arrive at Carolyn's home in Cleveland by twelve o'clock. Her home is a paradise. You better not speed. If you do, they will arrest you. You see, if they arrest you, you are sure to land in jail, and then you may not arrive in Cleveland at all.

You are just like a parrot. A parrot does not think. It just says everything it hears. The Arundel Band played carols during the Yuletide season. Harry is taking clarinet lessons. Did you see the big parade last night? I like the taste of caraway seeds.

# LESSON 60

| wa | war | qua | quar | wha | whar |

(Sound of "a" as in "all" and as short "o")

| wad | quart | wand | wart | squat |
| want | warn | quartz | wash | squash |
| warm | wasp | dwarf | squab | swab |
| swarm | squat | what | swamp | swan |
| thwart | war | watt | squad | wharf |
| wan | warp | ward | swatch | swap |
| was | quaff | watch | quash | swarm |
| | | | | |
| wallet | quarry | squadron | warrant | warranty |
| quadrant | wallop | swarthy | swatter | quadrille |
| warpath | quarter | wander | reward | water |
| quartet | squalor | quarrel | quality | quadruped |
| swatter | washing | wampum | warren | quandary |
| award | wardrobe | warden | quatrain | quadruplet |
| squander | wanton | quantum | squalid | quantity |

*Non-Phonic:* toward

## EXERCISES

What is war? War is a fight. We want no war, but if someone attacks us, we have to fight back to defend the land of the free. Today is fair and warm. In May it is somewhat warmer than in March. Walter gets up at seven. He washes his hands with soap in warm water. The best drink is milk; the next best is fresh water. Three quarters of the globe is covered with water. Some children drink a quart of milk every day.

# LESSON 60—(Continued)

"What are those long necked things swimming there in the water?" "Are they geese?" "No, they are called swans."

The farmer raises squash and brings it to the market to sell. When we want squash, we go to the market to buy it. To squash means to crush and flatten like a pancake.

When I went to market, I met Walter. He went eastward, while I went westward. Toward evening we met again, but this time Walter came westward and I went eastward. Let me see, what was it I wanted to buy in the shop on the mall? O, yes, I want a fly swatter. What is a fly swatter? We swat the fly with a fly swatter. To swat is to strike hard and kill the fly. I warn you not to go in the swamp. You will sink.

## WARNING: SWAMPY LAND. DO NOT DRIVE HERE.

### What Is It?

It has hands, but no arms, yet it strikes. It hangs on the wall, yet it goes. Seasons come and seasons go, yet it remains in the same spot.

(Clock)

Be helpful to others. You may need others to help you. As the saying goes, "One hand washes the other."

# REVIEW
## Long and Short Vowels

### Read Across 1

| | | |
|---|---|---|
| aim | - | am |
| paid | - | pad |
| maid | - | mad |
| rain | - | ran |
| main | - | man |
| laid | - | lad |
| claim | - | clam |
| brain | - | bran |
| plain | - | plan |
| Spain | - | span |

### Read Across 2

| | | |
|---|---|---|
| ate | - | at |
| hate | - | hat |
| fate | - | fat |
| tape | - | tap |
| rate | - | rat |
| lake | - | lack |
| Jake | - | Jack |
| bake | - | back |
| take | - | tack |
| sake | - | sack |

### Read Across 3

| | | |
|---|---|---|
| pair | - | par |
| fair | - | far |
| chair | - | char |
| stair | - | star |

### Read Across 4

| | | |
|---|---|---|
| bare | - | bar |
| care | - | car |
| stare | - | star |
| scare | - | scar |

### Read Across 5

| | | |
|---|---|---|
| ail | - | all |
| fail | - | fall |
| hail | - | hall |
| wail | - | wall |

### Read Across 6

| | | |
|---|---|---|
| gale | - | gall |
| tale | - | tall |
| bale | - | ball |
| stale | - | stall |

## REVIEW (Continued)
### Long and Short Vowels

| Read Across 1 | | | Read Across 2 | | |
|---|---|---|---|---|---|
| bead | - | bed | feel | - | fell |
| dean | - | den | meet | - | met |
| lead | - | led | weed | - | wed |
| neat | - | net | feed | - | fed |
| beat | - | bet | bleed | - | bled |
| read | - | red | steep | - | step |
| seal | - | sell | breed | - | bred |
| steam | - | stem | speed | - | sped |
| speak | - | speck | cheek | - | check |
| beast | - | best | freed | - | Fred |

| Read Across 3 | | | Read Across 4 | | | Read Across 5 | | |
|---|---|---|---|---|---|---|---|---|
| bite | - | bit | spine | - | spin | use | - | us |
| file | - | fill | prime | - | prim | tube | - | tub |
| pine | - | pin | like | - | lick | cute | - | cut |
| ripe | - | rip | pike | - | pick | fuse | - | fuss |
| mile | - | mill | slime | - | slim | cruise | - | crust |
| fight | - | fit | sight | - | sit | bruise | - | brusk |

| Read Across 6 | | | Read Across 7 | | | Read Across 8 | | |
|---|---|---|---|---|---|---|---|---|
| coat | - | cot | robe | - | rob | lyre | - | lynx |
| goat | - | got | note | - | not | tyke | - | tryst |
| road | - | rod | hope | - | hop | style | - | myth |
| bloat | - | blot | slope | - | slop | type | - | crypt |
| cloak | - | clock | stoke | - | stock | pyre | - | lynch |

## LONG AND SHORT VOWEL DRILL

| Read Across Column 1 | | | Read Across Column 2 | | |
|---|---|---|---|---|---|
| caned | - | canned | scared | - | scarred |
| hatter | - | hater | scraped | - | scrapped |
| backer | - | baker | staring | - | starring |
| later | - | latter | sparring | - | sparing |
| maiden | - | madden | stacked | - | staked |
| tacking | - | taking | bared | - | barred |
| falling | - | failing | cared | - | card |
| liked | - | licked | barley | - | barely |
| piker | - | picker | stripped | - | striped |
| ripper | - | riper | gripping | - | griping |
| miser | - | misser | spiting | - | spitting |
| tiled | - | tilled | platter | - | plater |
| filled | - | filed | slopped | - | sloped |
| biter | - | bitter | stoked | - | stocked |
| diner | - | dinner | staler | - | staller |
| hoping | - | hopping | scrapper | - | scraper |
| moped | - | mopped | starred | - | stared |
| robbed | - | robed | scaring | - | scarring |
| riding | - | ridding | steeped | - | stepped |
| ruder | - | rudder | severe | - | sever |
| holy | - | holly | fated | - | fatted |
| supper | - | super | steamed | - | stemmed |
| cutter | - | cuter | pining | - | pinning |

# LESSON 61

| or | - | oar | - | ore | - | our |

| | | | | |
|---|---|---|---|---|
| oar | ore | or | more | sore |
| cork | coarse | storm | store | porch |
| fork | tore | fourth | scorn | snore |
| Lord | form | course | board | stork |
| nor | horse | wore | born | for |
| shore | north | cord | worn | fort |
| swore | sort | hoarse | Ford | corn |
| torch | score | torn | horn | short |
| four | sworn | roar | thorn | port |
| hoard | yours | soar | court | gourd |

## DRILL

| | | | |
|---|---|---|---|
| sorely | shortly | sorest | horses |
| stormy | stored | import | torches |
| ashore | sorer | story | unborn |
| afford | deport | shortest | report |
| escort | assort | fourteenth | inform |
| explore | scornful | acorn | restore |
| horny | fourteen | export | corner |
| border | accord | recourse | aboard |

# LESSON 61—(Continued)

## EXERCISES

### A Short, Short Story

A weary, gray-haired man sat at a fork in the roads. His clothes seemed dusty and worn. There was not a button on his coat. It was just tied together with a cord. With his sore feet peeping from beneath his torn shoes, he was waiting for someone to come along and direct him on his way.

Shortly after, a lad, no more than fourteen, came along hopping and whistling. The man beckoned to him and said hoarsely, "Son, which one of these roads leads to the shore?" "Well," said the youth after thinking for a moment, "the one to your right is the shorter, but longer, and the one to the left is longer, but shorter."

"Why do you speak with such scorn, son? Or are you trying to poke fun at me?"

"I beg your pardon, my dear man. I spoke the truth. You see, the road on the right is the shorter, but full of marshes, swamps, and thorn bushes. Therefore, it will take you longer. The one to the left is longer, but straight and paved, and on it, it will take a shorter time to reach the shore."

"Thanks a lot," said the man. "You are surely very smart. The Lord bless you!"

We eat in order that we may live, but we do not live in order that we shall eat.

"He who plants thorns must not expect to gather roses."

# LESSON 62

## "er" sound

| er | ir | ur | yr | our | ear followed by a consonant |
|---|---|---|---|---|---|
| te**r**m | bi**r**d | cu**r**l | mart**yr** | j**our**ney | **ear**th |

| | | | |
|---|---|---|---|
| per | jerk | serve | clerk |
| her | nerve | berth | herd |
| err | stern | fern | perch |
| | | | |
| dirt | chirp | firm | girl |
| birth | third | first | flirt |
| skirt | squirt | thirst | sir |
| stir | fir | quirk | whirl |
| | | | |
| cur | furl | hurl | hurt |
| fur | turn | burnt | burst |
| slur | curse | nurse | purse |
| urn | burn | curb | churn |
| church | lurk | lurch | purl |
| | | | |
| Byrd | satyr | martyr | myrrh |
| | | | |
| journal | flourish | nourish | courtesy |
| | | | |
| earn | dearth | pearl | search |
| heard | yearn | hearse | learn |

## LESSON 62—(Continued)

## DRILL

| dirty | curly | early | firmer | kernel |
| firmly | affirm | girlish | unfurl | conserve |
| thirty | Thursday | deserve | hurtful | Saturday |
| thirsty | murder | servant | unhurt | obverse |
| alert | reserve | reverse | infirm | skirmish |
| peruse | pursue | observe | perform | murmur |

*Non-Phonic:* were  answer  purpose
*Exception:* beard

### or and ar slurred like er

| labor | favor | armor | collar |
| vapor | humor | horror | polar |
| sailor | traitor | pastor | beggar |
| tailor | flavor | parlor | altar |
| razor | doctor | dollar | mortar |
| victor | solar | rancor | molar |
| pillar | actor | succor | pallor |
|  | attorney | stubborn |  |

## EXERCISES

On Sunday we all go to church. The church is on the corner of Thirty-Third Street in a suburb of Richmond. The man who preaches the sermon is called a parson. Doctor Herbert, the parson, says that to err is to sin. To err also means to make a mistake.

Sometimes we call a turkey a bird. A turkey has wings, but does not chirp or fly like a bird. A Turk is a person who was born of Turkish parents.

# LESSON 62—(Continued)

I heard that Ernest was hurt. The nurse gave him first aid. Ernest has a sister whose name is Pearl. Pearl has dark, curly hair. Pearl is a very sweet girl, and we all love her.

In Pearl's club there are thirteen girls. All of the thirteen girls learn useful trades, so they can earn money to buy the things they need. They meet every first and third Thursday of each month. Pearl will have her thirteenth birthday next Thursday. Her mother will bake a birthday cake to serve at the party and will purchase a purse as a gift for her. She will invite all the girls in her club. Pearl deserves to be loved by everybody. She is a fine person. Her report card always has all A's. She leads her class every term.

Ernest is an air pilot. It takes strong nerves to fly an airplane. He used to be a clerk in a drug store. There he learned that "early to bed and early to rise" is very wise. He also learned that when thirsty, the best drink is a glass of fresh water. He says, "Don't flirt with fire, you'll get burnt." Ernest's pal Bernard is an attorney.

This is a tailor-made suit. It was made to order. The labor for a tailor-made suit costs more. In a dollar, there are four quarters. A quarter is a fourth part of a dollar.

When I came into the barber shop to get a hair cut, there were four men waiting: a sailor, a tailor, a doctor, and a pastor. The sailor was first. The tailor was to be next, but the pastor asked the sailor to do him a favor and let him go first. "True," he said, "first come first served, but a bride is waiting for me to marry her to her chosen one. The wedding will be at the altar of the church." The tailor was to be next, but the doctor pleaded with him. He said, "I just had a call. A girl has broken her collar bone and I must rush."

While they were waiting, a beggar came in and said, "Brother, can you spare some money, please? I am hungry." We were all astir, reaching into our pockets for our purses. The tailor remarked, "If I had had my hair cut when it was my turn, I'd have saved a quarter." "Yes," said the doctor with his pleasing humor, "but you have done a good deed valued more highly than dollars. It is far better to give than to take."

# LESSON 63

| wor sounded as wer |

| work | word | world |
| worse | worst | worth |
| | worm | |

| works | worlds | worldly | worry |
| worms | wormy | worthy | working |
| worked | wording | workers | worship |

*Exceptions:* worn  sworn
*Non-Phonic:* sword

## EXERCISES

Mr. Earl Wadsworth is a farmer. He served in the World War as a sailor. Sailing the seven seas, he was all over the world. After the war, he went back to his farm, which was given to him by his parents. He works on the farm from early in the morning until late at night. There is plenty of work to do at all seasons of the year. In the winter as well as in the summer, and in the fall as well as in the spring, he is at work.

Mr. Wadsworth has these mottoes: "Whatever is worthwhile doing at all, is worth doing well," and "A bird in hand is worth two in the bush." "The early bird catches the worm." To him the hardest work is to do nothing. He says that the Lord made hands for us to work with. In his orchard, there are many fruit trees: plum, cherry, peach, and many other fruit trees. He takes care of them by spraying, so the worms will not eat the leaves and blossoms. Worms do much harm to plants, trees, and fruit.

Even on Sunday he rises early, but he does not work. On Sunday he only attends to the horses and the other live stock. After they are fed, he puts on his best clothes, and he and his wife and children go to

## LESSON 63—(Continued)

church to worship. He says work and worship keep the world in order. "Be careful with your words," he says. "A word may hurt more than a slap."

When one wants to learn, but can't learn quickly, that is bad. One who can learn, but does not want to learn is worse, but one who can't learn and does not want to learn is the worst off.

## LESSON 64

### Seven sounds of ea

#### 1. ea like long e (most prevalent sound)

| beat | seat | heat |
| fear | near | seal |
| deacon | mean | treaty |

#### 2. ea like short e

| bread | lead | deaf | threat |
| tread | dread | death | head |
| sweat | thread | read | stead |
| dead | breath | health | wealth |
| meant | stealth | realm | breast |

#### 3. ea like long a

| break | great | yea | steak | breakers |
| breaking | greatly | breaks | greater | greatest |

## LESSON 64—(Continued)

### 4. ear like air

| bear    | pear  | swear    | wear  | tear    |
|---------|-------|----------|-------|---------|
| bearing | pears | swearing | wears | tearing |

### 5. ear like ar

| heart  | hearth      | hearken   |
|--------|-------------|-----------|
| hearty | hearthstone | heartless |

### 6. ear like er
(See Lesson 62.)

| heard | learn | pearl    | dearth  | search |
|-------|-------|----------|---------|--------|
|       | early | rehearse | earnest |        |

### 7. ea—both sounded

| area    | create   | reassure   | ethereal   |
|---------|----------|------------|------------|
| idea    | theater  | deactivate | reality    |
| althea  | meander  | reaffirm   | delineate  |
| react   | readjust | oleander   | reactivate |

## DRILL

| deathly   | headed   | leaden     | treading |
| reread    | dreaded  | healthy    | unread   |
| steady    | instead  | threaten   | wealthy  |
| ready     | sweater  | breathless | feather  |
| leather   | weather  | heaven     | heavy    |
| breakfast | threaded | deafness   | pleasant |
| sweating  | weapon   | healthful  | ahead    |

# LESSON 64—(Continued)

## EXERCISES

A baker bakes bread. He makes bread from wheat, rye, and corn. The baker works steadily all night so the bread will be ready early for breakfast and for sandwiches for lunch. A great many of us have to sweat to earn our daily bread. A person who is not ready to do his share of work or is not steady at his task is called a slacker. "Early to bed and early to rise makes a man healthy, wealthy, and wise."

A person who cannot hear is deaf, but he who can hear, but does not want to hear is worse than deaf. One does not need to be wealthy to be healthy and happy. Health and wealth do not go hand in hand. Milk is a pleasant and healthful drink.

Mr. Irving Barker is a big game hunter. He hunts for bears and tigers. He was ready to leave at daybreak this morning, but the weather was very bad. Instead, he will leave next Thursday if the weather permits. Mr. Barker is a heavy set but healthy man, bright as a silver dollar, with steady hands and keen eyes. When he goes on a hunting trip, he is dressed warmly in a heavy sweater over which he wears a short leather coat. The leather belt is packed chock-full of bullets for easy reach. On his head he wears a fur cap and on his hands, fur-lined gloves. His weapons, three or four shotguns, are clean and shining brightly.

One who makes leather is called a tanner. Leather is made of hides. Bullets are made from lead. Lead is a metal which has many uses. We call pistols, guns, and cannons weapons. The head, breast, and heart are parts of the body. A person lives while the heart beats in his breast. When the heart stops beating, it means death. A person who has no life in him is dead. Not every person who is big is great. "Birds of a feather flock together."

# LESSON 65

**o** and **ou**
(Like **u** in r**u**de or in p**u**t)

| o and ou like u in rude |        |         |       |       | o like u in put |
|-------------------------|--------|---------|-------|-------|-----------------|
| do    | route | lose    | wound | who   | wolf   |
| to    | soup  | crouton | prove | whom  | wolves |
| move  | shoe  | group   | croup | whose | bosom  |
|       |       |         |       |       | woman  |

## DRILL

| moved  | loser   | louver | proved  | disproved  |
| moving | proving | doing  | losing  | disapproved |
| routed | nougat  | coupon | removed | wounded    |

*Non-Phonic:*   women   two

## EXERCISES

The bosom is the breast. Men's clothes have bosom or inside pockets. Women's clothes have no bosom pockets. Shirley said, "Today women are equal to men in everything."

That woman has proved herself worthy of love. She is the mother of two children for whom she lives and works. Her husband is a sickly man. He can't earn a living. It is she alone who works to keep the wolf away from her home. She does not want to lose her husband, so she is doing the work of two. She hopes he will improve and regain his health and do his part again as he used to do. In the meantime, she has to do it all by herself. And there is plenty to do to keep the four in shoes and clothes and pay for eats and rent.

## LESSON 65—(Continued)

They moved into this block two months ago. The rent here is cheaper, and this is nearer to the store where she works. She saves the bus fare. She is losing much sleep, but she can't afford to lose any time, for when she comes home from the shoe store where she is a saleswoman, she has to serve supper, wash, scrub, and mend. Yes, and she even has to make some soup for the next day. She proves that "where there is a will, there is a way."

## LESSON 66

| **fore-** (in front, before, ahead, first) | | **for-** (away, completely, prohibit, refusal, neglect) | |
|---|---|---|---|
| foreman | forefront | forget | forever |
| foretell | forestall | forgot | formal |
| foresee | forefathers | forbid | forlorn |
| forecast | forebode | forgive | fortress |
| forearm | forerunner | forgave | fortune |
| forehead | foresight | forsake | forward |
| foreword | foretaste | format | forgo |

## EXERCISES

The person who directs the workmen is called the foreman. The foreman tells the workmen what to do. The part between the hair of the head and the eyes is the forehead.

"What is the weather forecast for today?" "Fair and warmer." To forecast is to foretell. There are things we must never forget, and there are things it is best to forget. We must never forget to respect the rights of others. To forget and forgive harm and hurt done to us is godly.

## LESSON 66—(Continued)

Tommy used to forget where he put his things when he went to sleep. One night he made a note saying: "My shoes are under the bed. The socks are in the shoes. My shirt and tie are on the chair, and I am in the bed." He put the note in his pocket and tied a string on his finger not to forget where he put the note. When he woke up in the morning, the string was on his finger, but he forgot why it was there. After thinking hard and long, he searched his pockets and to his great delight there was the note. He read it. "Shoes under the bed." Right. "Socks in the shoes." Yes, there they are. "The shirt and tie on the chair." Right again. "I am in bed." Well, let's see. He turned the blankets and the sheets over, but he was not there. "Oh, dear me!" he yelled in despair. "Where am I?"

To foretell is to tell what will happen before it happens. One who can foresee is said to have foresight. A person may not foretell what may happen. Yet, if he is smart, he will foresee it. To forgive is to pardon. Forgave is the past tense of forgive. "I pray Thee, O Lord, forsake me not," means "Please do not leave me." We all must strive to go forward. To march forward is to go ahead.

## LESSON 67

| **per-** (through, over, away, completely) | **pre-** (before) | **pro-** (instead of, for, forward) |
|---|---|---|
| perfect | prefer | proclaim |
| perform | prepare | profane |
| perfume | pretend | profess |
| perhaps | prevent | propel |
| permit | preserve | protect |
| person | present | protest |

## LESSON 67—(Continued)

| | | |
|---|---|---|
| pertain | prefix | promote |
| permute | prelude | prorate |
| perplex | preplan | protrude |
| persist | predate | program |
| perspire | prewar | prolong |
| pervade | preside | profile |

## EXERCISES

Hope for the best, but prepare for the worst. At all times and at all costs perform your task and duty. We prefer a person who is the least among the great rather than one who is the leader among the least. The truly great prefer wisdom before wealth. Be real, be true, and be right rather than pretend to be what you are not. No one can be perfect, but at least we must try to be as nearly perfect as we can.

Permit is just the reverse of forbid. "I permit you" means you may do a thing, but "I forbid you" means you must not do it. Protect and preserve your health and prevent sickness. The wise prepare today to have something for the days to come. Take a lesson and learn from the ant. The ant prepares in the summer so she may have something to eat in the winter. Today is the present, the next day is a secret. Perhaps means it may or may not happen. When you have a duty to perform, don't say, "I shall do it later." Perhaps "later" may never come.

Happy are those who are content with what they have. The contents of this box will melt. Keep it away from the heat. Before you go hunting, you must first secure a permit. "Have you a permit to drive a car?" "No, sir, but please permit me to park my car here while I go to get a permit."

All members of the club will be present when I present the speaker of the evening to them. After the meeting we shall present the speaker with a costly present. If you are tardy again, I'll refuse to excuse you. Do not leave refuse on the grass in the park. We refuse to pick up the refuse unless it is left in a trash can. One who rebels is a rebel. To rebel is to rise in protest against someone.

# LESSON 68

**-le**

(Read Across)          (Read Across)

| maple | - | apple | idle | - | middle |
| ladle | - | saddle | Bible | - | dimple |
| fable | - | fiddle | trifle | - | thimble |
| stable | - | sample | bridle | - | brittle |
| ogle | - | nozzle | scruple | - | shuttle |

## DRILL

| able | drizzle | juggle | peddle | rumble |
| angle | eagle | jingle | pebble | simple |
| ankle | frizzle | kettle | pimple | steeple |
| beetle | gamble | little | pickle | sizzle |
| battle | giggle | meddle | puddle | stumble |
| bugle | gargle | muzzle | puzzle | settle |
| bubble | grumble | noble | purple | scuttle |
| bottle | griddle | nibble | myrtle | sprinkle |
| cable | huddle | needle | wobble | temple |
| cattle | jumble | nipple | rattle | tremble |
| cradle | jungle | paddle | rumple | tumble |
| trample | scramble | warble | marble | turtle |
| rifle | axle | tangle | bundle | struggle |
| buckle | smuggle | table | straddle | scribble |

## LESSON 68—(Continued)

### -le — three-or-more-syllable words

| | | | |
|---|---|---|---|
| flexible | article | gullible | responsible |
| barnacle | tentacle | quenchable | obtainable |
| lovable | capable | sensible | presentable |
| livable | syllable | pinnacle | reasonable |
| possible | particle | tractable | remarkable |

### Suffixing -le words

(Read Across)

- stifle - stifling
- able - ably
- staple - stapler
- idle - idleness
- whittle - whittled

(Read Across)

- settle - settlement
- purple - purplish
- simple - simplest
- waffle - waffles
- noble - nobleman

*Exceptions:* triple treble
*Non-Phonic:* people

## EXERCISES

A gray haired man was standing on a street corner bare headed in the drizzling rain waiting for someone to pass by and tell him what street it was. Many people passed by, but he was ashamed to ask them. At last a little girl came along. The man said to her, "Little girl, will you please tell me if this is Maple Street?" "Mister," she said, "can't you read what it says right over your head?" "O yes, yes. But I forgot my eyeglasses, and I can't see." "Hm, and what do you have on your nose?" "Why these—these are not reading glasses." "Then why

## LESSON 68—(Continued)

do you wear them? Besides, the letters up there are as big as my fist, and there are only two words, and not a whole crossword puzzle." "To my great shame, I must confess that I never learned to read." "I am sorry," said the little girl, "but you spoke in riddles. This is Maple Street all right."

Mr. Brittle lives on the northeast corner, Mr. Steeple lives on the northwest corner, and Mr. York lives in the middle of the block. All three men served in the World War. Mr. Brittle was first to settle here on this estate. He raises cattle and has many fine horses in his stable. He is able to ride any horse bareback with only a bridle. Only seldom does he use a saddle.

Mr. Steeple, with many battle scars on his body and a broken ankle, is not able to do much. Yet he is never idle. He attends to his apple orchard and peddles fruit. In his spare time, he plays the fiddle or reads the Bible. He leads a simple but very happy life. He does not swear, drink, or gamble. You never hear him grumble. His wife, a plain woman with a noble heart, has no time to meddle in other people's affairs. She lives for her husband and children.

She prepares three wholesome meals every day and makes griddle cakes and apple pies. When the washing and cleaning are done, you'll see her with a thimble on her finger and a needle in her hand mending socks and repairing overalls. In the middle she hears something sizzling on the stove. It is the bottle and nipple for the baby. The water bubbles in the kettle. Then she tells her children a bedtime story or a fable, and so another day passes in the worthwhile struggle.

# LESSON 69

**-ind** and **-ild**

Words with Long I

Ending in Two Consonants Without a Second Vowel

| bind  | grind | rind  | wild  | blind |
| mind  | find  | mild  | hind  | child |
|       |       | kind  |       |       |

## DRILL

| binding   | minded    | behind    | finder    |
| kindly    | kindness  | unkind    | mindful   |
| winding   | blindly   | blindness | grinder   |
| mildly    | milder    | mildest   | mildness  |
| wilder    | wildest   | childish  | remind    |
| childless | findings  | mankind   | hindsight |

*Exception:* gild
*Sound of i both long and short:* wind

## EXERCISES

There are many kinds of wild beasts in the jungle. A jungle is a forest of trees and tall, wild grass. A wolf and a tiger are wild beasts. Native-born tribes in jungle areas find ways of coping with life in those wild thickets.

## LESSON 69—(Continued)

A blind person cannot see at all. The blind grope in the dark, even in the daytime. Yet they can find their way by feeling with their hands or with a cane. Some blind people use a trained dog to lead them. A dog trained to lead the blind is called a "seeing eye" dog. Some people are born blind; others are struck with blindness later in life. At all times we must bear in mind to deal kindly with the blind.

Mrs. Wilder lost her purse. She put an ad in the paper which read: "Lost, purse with ten single dollar bills, three quarters, two dimes, one penny, and a key. Finder please return. Reward."

Mr. Wilder is a lens grinder. He grinds lenses for eyeglasses and watch crystals. To grind means to grate. We rub an ax against a stone to sharpen it. The green part of a watermelon is the rind. The bark of a tree is its rind. To bind means to tie or to fasten. The blacksmith had to bind the hind feet of the horse when he shod it for the first time. The hind feet are the two back feet of the horse. Anything that is not strong, sharp, wild, or harsh is said to be mild. Mild weather or a mild winter is not severe.

Miss Binder, my child's teacher, says, "I find that you must not be kind to a child who does not mind. If you always have to be behind him and remind him to do his homework, he will fail." To fail means to be behind in your grade. Teacher: "Jennie, name ten wild animals." Jennie: "Five wolves and five bears."

# LESSON 70

**-old**  **-olt**  **-ost**  **-oll**

**Words with Long O
Ending in Two Consonants Without a Second Vowel**

| old  | cold  | fold | gold   |
|------|-------|------|--------|
| bold | hold  | mold | sold   |
| told | scold | jolt | bolt   |
| colt | post  | most | host   |
|      | molt  | volt |        |

| toll  | poll  | roll | stroll |
|-------|-------|------|--------|
| droll | troll | boll | scroll |

**More-Than-One-Syllable Root Words
Ending in -ol Having Long O Sound**

**Double L When Adding Suffix Beginning with a Vowel**

(Read Across)

| Root Word | Sound of O Remains Long When Adding Suffixes |
|-----------|----------------------------------------------|
| control   | - controlling, controller, controllable, controlled |
| extol     | - extolled, extoller, extolling, extolment  |
| patrol    | - patroller, patrolling, patrolled, patrolman |

## LESSON 70—(Continued)

## DRILL

| older | coldest | unfold | golden |
| boldly | holder | folding | scolded |
| untold | poster | mostly | almost |
| retold | hostess | strolling | roller |
| foretold | scolding | jolted | foremost |
| provost | folder | swollen | enroll |
| tolling | pollster | molten | stroller |

*Exceptions:* doll   loll   moll   lost   cost   frost

## EXERCISES

Gold is a bright, shiny metal. But everything that glitters is not gold. Goldfish live in cold water. There is an old saying, "Don't spill the impure water before you get pure water." This means, "Hold on to what you have."

Most people in the world wish to live long, but never to feel old. You are as old as you feel. The older some people get, the smarter they are. According to the poll taken last month, most of the people in this area are in favor of building the proposed toll road. Toll is a tax or duty we pay for the right to pass over a public road.

The teacher calls the roll in the morning. If a child is not present at roll call, he is marked absent or tardy. For being tardy, the teacher will scold you, and for being absent, you are told to bring a note. They also call the roll every day in the army and navy. After the roll call, each man goes to his post.

In the army camps, almost anywhere you turn, you see a poster on the wall. On the posters you read the orders of the day or you are told what to do or where to go. The men serving Uncle Sam are trained to be bold. Bold means fearless. Uncle Sam is the best uncle, and his men are the boldest and best fighters in the world. They don't get cold feet, but hold fast to old glory, the red, white, and blue. The flags with the stars and stripes fly high at every post.

# LESSON 71

## Three-Syllable Words

### Double Suffixes

| 1 | 2 | 3 |
|---|---|---|
| play-ful-ly | use-ful-ness | { lov/e-ing-ly |
| faithfully | hatefulness | { lovingly |
| gratefully | faithfulness | smilingly |
| cheerfully | cheerfulness | willingly |
| spitefully | helpfulness | seemingly |
| skillfully | restfulness | { penny/-i-less |
| painlessly | watchfulness | { penniless |
| aimlessly | recklessness | dutiful |
| fearlessly | fearlessness | holiness |
| endlessly | sleeplessness | happily |
| spotlessly | uselessness | easily |
| recklessly | restlessness | lazily |
| tactlessly | helplessness | happiness |
| selfishly | childishness | worldliness |

## DRILL

| | | | |
|---|---|---|---|
| bakery | analyze | enemy | bravery |
| slavery | usual | ignorant | alcohol |
| memory | existed | displeasing | personal |
| melody | wondering | family | personnel |
| openly | covering | different | supervise |
| unity | divided | carpenter | implement |

## LESSON 71—(Continued)

| | | | |
|---|---|---|---|
| miserly | eskimo | barbecue | miracle |
| dynasty | colloquy | dynamite | worthiness |
| September | October | November | important |
| Washington | luckily | kindliness | armory |
| yesterday | holiday | together | enrollment |
| blissfully | wistfulness | harmlessness | handicapped |

*Non-Phonic:* Wednesday

## LESSON 72

> Sound **c soft** as **s**
>
> When **c** is followed by **e, i,** or **y,** it has the sound of **s**.
> (c's name sound)

**ce**

| | | | | |
|---|---|---|---|---|
| ace | grace | mice | cell | thrice |
| lace | brace | vice | cent | peace |
| place | trace | nice | scene | since |
| pace | ice | slice | scent | mince |
| race | dice | twice | force | hence |
| face | lice | price | farce | fence |
| space | rice | cease | spice | chance |
| spruce | glance | dance | prince | splice |
| quince | source | truce | juice | prance |

## LESSON 72—(Continued)

## DRILL

### After **soft c, e** is sounded in **-es**

| | | | |
|---|---|---|---|
| cement | notice | recess | offices |
| recent | decent | police | replace |
| unlace | reduce | grocer | census |
| license | justice | grocery | embraces |
| laced | laces | forces | paces |
| raced | races | bracer | tracer |
| nicest | slices | prices | spices |
| nicely | graceful | peaceful | princess |
| disgrace | parcel | advance | entrance |
| center | ulcer | crevice | romances |
| abscess | nuisance | resources | lettuce |

*Non-Phonic:* scarce   once   recipe   soccer
circuit   corpuscle   muscle

## EXERCISES

Once, on a late winter night, a fox, who was very hungry, decided to have a nice chicken dinner. He raced up to a nearby farm, but alas, a high fence was in the way of his goal. He paced and danced back and forth to find a hole to enter, but there was not a trace of any open space. With all his might, he pushed at the gate to force it open, but that was bolted. "This is the place to get a bite all right," he said licking his lips. "I'll just take a chance and jump over the fence."

The great, faithful watchdog in the barnyard scented the enemy but did not stir. "Silence is golden," he mused. This was no

## LESSON 72—(Continued)

time to bark. He just cocked up his ears and lay in wait. The fox leaped; the old fence swayed and rattled. He glanced over the scene and noticed the dog. He'd have been glad to jump back to freedom again, but was held fast by the barbed wire.

He made a face like a saint and began to preach. "Peace, peace on earth, peace be with you all," he said. "I came to tell you that the time has arrived when strife shall cease. Henceforth there shall be justice and peace, and no malice at all. Come, dear chickens and hens, come over here. Let's embrace and live peacefully together." "That was a very nice speech," said an old hen to the fox, "but if you speak the truth, why do you sit on the fence? Descend and come to us."

"Hm—yes, every word I said is true, I swear. You can even find it in the Bible, but I am afraid I can't trust that dog. A dog thinks evil and is full of vice. He won't take my word for it, and he refuses to read the Bible."

## LESSON 73

**ci**      **cy**

| | | | |
|---|---|---|---|
| city | civil | cigar | cider |
| citron | cinder | decide | incite |
| recite | acid | pencil | scissors |
| icing | lacing | dancing | circus |
| Pacific | circular | civic | vaccinate |
| accident | icicle | circle | incidence |
| vicinity | excitement | participate | exercise |
| fancy | icy | mercy | juicy |
| spicy | spacy | cycle | cynic |
| scythe | infancy | policy | privacy |
| bicycles | vacancy | decency | tendency |
| cylinder | cyst | cymbal | cybernetics |

## LESSON 73—(Continued)

## DRILL

| | | | |
|---|---|---|---|
| according | civilize | crescent | cancelled |
| concerts | December | commerce | circulate |
| accused | tobacco | accepted | concept |
| accede | acclaiming | citizen | concrete |
| access | success | accident | contract |
| occur | accustom | convince | except |
| electric | succeed | convict | cigarette |
| accent | exceeding | cygnet | according |
| proceed | precede | embracing | embraceable |
| convincing | precedence | vaccine | successfully |
| accessory | danceable | precise | accidentally |

*Abbreviation:* etc. = *et cetera (meaning "and others"; "and so forth")*
*Non-Phonic:* cyclone

## EXERCISES

The highest officer in this city is the mayor. The mayor's office is in the City Hall. Almost every street in the city has concrete pavement. Concrete is made of cement, gravel, and sand. Concrete makes a hard surface. At night the streets are lit by electric lights. In certain places where there is no electricity, they use gas lights.

The city has an excellent police force. A policeman on the force is called an officer. The police officers patrol the streets day and night. They are always on the watch for indecent people who are bent on committing crimes. A person accused of robbing, stealing, or breaking the traffic rules is arrested. Some officers ride in police cars. Others ride motorcycles in order to be able to get to the scene of the crime or accident quickly.

# LESSON 73—(Continued)

We also have a fire department in the city. The main post office and its branch offices are in the city, but are not city property. The post office takes care of the mail. A postal clerk must pass a civil service test and wait until a vacancy occurs. Then he is called to fill the vacancy.

There is a city children's clinic and a dental clinic for those who cannot pay the doctor's or dentist's fee. In the clinic they treat the sick, fix teeth, and vaccinate.

We have many department stores, grocery stores, and drug stores in the city. In a department store you can buy almost anything you may want from a pencil and scissors to a bicycle. The grocer sells fancy fruit, fruit juices, sweet cider, ice cream, icy drinks, cigars, tobacco, cigarettes, and all kinds of spices, like pepper, celery salt, cinnamon, etc. Every store must have a city license. Most stores are open every day except Sunday. Some stores are open every day in the week.

We have many amusement places, dance halls, parks, and lakes. In the month of December the lakes are frozen stiff and we go ice skating. In the winter we go to hear music concerts, and in the spring and summer we go to see the circus. Florence goes to a music concert whenever one is billed in this vicinity.

In the United States, we have democracy, freedom, and peace. We want quality citizens, not quantity voters.

# LESSON 74

**ci as sh**

**ci** followed by a vowel = **sh**
(Not in first syllable of root word)

### cial as shul, shal

| | |
|---|---|
| social | crucial |
| special | superficial |
| specialist | commercial |
| official | beneficial |
| officially | financial |
| judicial | racial |
| artificial | racially |

### cian as shun, shan

| | |
|---|---|
| Grecian | politician |
| optician | electricians |
| musicians | statistician |

### cient as shunt, shent

| | |
|---|---|
| deficient | proficient |
| efficient | sufficient |
| efficiently | liquefacient |

### ciency as shunsee, shensee

| | |
|---|---|
| deficiency | proficiency |
| efficiency | sufficiency |

### cious as shus

| | |
|---|---|
| gracious | suspicious |
| graciousness | delicious |
| luscious | malicious |
| conscious | atrocious |
| consciously | unconscious |
| ferocious | loquacious |
| precious | precocious |
| vicious | tenacious |
| avaricious | fallacious |

### ci as shee
### vowel after ci sounded

| | |
|---|---|
| ex-officio | fiduciary |
| indicia | beneficiary |

### ci as sh
### (miscellaneous)

| | |
|---|---|
| species | sociable |
| glacier | unsociable |
| suspicion | Lucius |
| conscience | Marcia |

## LESSON 74—(Continued)

| ciate as "she ate" | | ce as sh |
|---|---|---|
| associate | excruciate | (Occasionally, spelling will be ce instead of ci.) |
| officiate | excruciating | |
| appreciate | emaciate | |
| depreciate | emaciated | |

| | | |
|---|---|---|
| | ocean | vinaceous |
| | curvaceous | saponaceous |

*Exceptions:* society  financier
*Non-Phonic:* ancient

*NOTE:* **-ous** ending indicates adjective
**-us** ending indicates noun
**-an** ending indicates person, adjective, or geographical location

### EXERCISES

Anything not real is artificial. The dentists make artificial teeth. Electric light is an artificial light. Regular and special airplanes fly to Washington daily. The President travels on a special airplane. One who grinds lenses or fits eyeglasses is an optician. The Grecians are an ancient people. One born in Greece of Greek parents is a Grecian. Ancient means anything with a very old history. A kind and noble person with a clean conscience is gracious.

The queen is a gracious lady. As a rule, the highest official in a city is the mayor. The highest elected official in the United States is the President. The wedding of Miss Alice Price to Dr. Cecil Tracy will take place on Wednesday, December twenty-fifth, in the Grace Church. Reverend Herbert Prince will officiate. After the ceremony, the bridal party will be entertained in the spacious Grecian Hall, where delicious refreshments will be served. The wedding will be a great social event.

To officiate is to perform or to do the duty of office. Spacious means a place with plenty of space. Delicious means tasty. Mr. Lacy, who played last night at the concert, is a very proficient musician. We

## LESSON 74—(Continued)

appreciate and greatly value his work. Proficient means expert in his line. A musician is one who plays music skillfully.

All the wiring and electrical work in this church were done by an efficient electrician. "Tell me with whom you associate, and I'll tell you who you are," means that if you chum with malicious and vicious people, that is sufficient reason to be suspicious that you are no better than they are. To associate with right-minded people is very beneficial. A worthy, gracious person is more precious than gold.

## LESSON 75

**ti as sh**
ti followed by a vowel = **sh**
(Not in first syllable of root word)

### tion as shun

| | |
|---|---|
| nation | distortion |
| notion | addition |
| motioned | ambition |
| portion | munitions |
| action | condition |
| section | position |
| mentioning | location |
| station | attention |
| stationary | educational |
| stationery | invitation |
| relationship | imitation |
| vacationer | explanation |
| election | application |
| solution | reflection |
| depletion | conjunction |
| projection | persecution |
| constitution | contortion |

### tian as shun, shan

| | |
|---|---|
| titian | dietitian |
| Martian | |

### tial as shul, shal

| | |
|---|---|
| initial | impartial |
| partial | influential |
| impartial | sequential |
| essential | differential |
| credential | nuptials |
| prudential | interstitial |
| potential | inconsequential |

### tious as shus

| | |
|---|---|
| surreptitious | nutritious |
| pretentious | fictitious |
| ostentatious | captious |

## LESSON 75—(Continued)

### tient as shunt, shent

patient    quotient

### tiate as "she ate"

satiate          differentiate
substantiate    ingratiate
initiate         expatiate
negotiate       novitiate

*Exceptions: patio   frontier*

### ti as sh (miscellaneous)

penitentiary    initiative
patience        ratio
nasturtium      impartiality
inertia         solatium
in absentia     expatiation

**After s, sound ti as ch.**

### tion, tian as chun tial as chul

Christian      question
combustion    bestial

## EXERCISES

This is the greatest nation on earth. It is the most blessed nation, a nation made up of many races who came here to live in peace and harmony. We are ruled by a constitution. The "Declaration of Independence" and the United States Constitution are the two most precious things we have.

In November of every fourth year, there is a national election. The presidential election takes place at the national election, when we elect a president and a vice-president. In the summer before an election, each party holds a convention to which every state in the union sends a delegation. Each delegate to the convention must present his credentials. The selection and nomination of candidates for the presidency are decided at the national conventions.

Most of the city population live in the residential sections. That portion of the city is farthest from a railroad terminal. City dwellers must have police protection.

## LESSON 75—(Continued)

A person who wants to become a policeman must make application for the position. In his application he must mention his occupation and education. In addition, he must pass a health examination. He must take instruction unquestioningly from the higher officer and have no objections. It is his duty to perform his obligations, under all conditions, according to police regulations. Every public celebration is under police direction.

If he has ambition and patience and pays attention to his work faithfully, he is due a promotion.

## LESSON 76

**si as sh and zh**     **xi as k-sh**

**si followed by a vowel = sh or zh**
(Not in first syllable of root word)

| After a consonant, sound si as sh ||  | After r, sound |
|---|---|---|---|
| ssion as shun || sion as shun | sion as zhun, shun |
| mission | depression | expansion | version |
| omission | aggression | revulsion | diversion |
| commission | profession | extension | excursion |
| permission | confession | convulsion | aversion |
| submission | succession | dissension | conversion |
| oppression | procession | compulsion | submersion |
| concussion | discussion | dimension | reversion |
| impression | recession | expulsion | inversion |
| possession | compression | suspension | subversion |
| expression | digression | mansion | incursion |

158

## LESSON 76—(Continued)

### After a vowel, sound si as zh
#### sion as zhun

| | |
|---|---|
| vision | decision |
| division | explosion |
| revision | illusion |
| occasion | confusion |
| invasion | conclusion |
| provision | supervision |
| seclusion | delusion |
| adhesion | transfusion |
| lesion | division |
| abrasion | television |

### si as zh and sh
#### (miscellaneous)

| | |
|---|---|
| hosiery | Asia |
| transient | Asian |
| transience | Polynesia |
| magnesia | Polynesian |
| anesthesia | Indonesia |
| amnesia | Indonesian |
| dyspepsia | Micronesia |
| fantasia | Micronesian |
| dyscrasia | Russia |
| artesian | Russian |

### xi as k-sh

#### xion as k-shun

| | |
|---|---|
| complexion | flexion |
| crucifixion | fluxion |

#### xious as k-shus

noxious
obnoxious
anxious

### su as shu and zhu
(Long u construction)

#### su as shu

| | |
|---|---|
| sure | sensual |
| assure | insurance |
| insure | issue |
| censure | tissue |
| fissure | pressure |
| sugar | sugary |
| surety | issuance |

#### After a vowel, su as zhu

| | | |
|---|---|---|
| pleasure | enclosure | treasury |
| treasure | exposure | foreclosure |
| measure | disclosure | closure |
| usury | usual | unusual |
| usurious | pleasurable | measurement |
| treasurer | measurable | usurer |

# LESSON 76—(Continued)

## EXERCISES

The doctor said that the patient needs diversion. The patient must get away from his work for a day or two every week. The doctor advised a weekly excursion as the best diversion. It was hard to make the decision, but finally the patient came to the conclusion that it was best to take the doctor's advice.

To drive a car, one must have perfect vision; that is, perfect eyesight. To see ahead of time, or a dream, is also a vision. The act of dividing is also called division. A child learns addition before he can learn division.

The procession was headed east under the supervision of the funeral director, when suddenly we heard an explosion, or rather several explosions in quick succession. The frightened people were in great confusion, and police had to order suspension of traffic for some time. Procession is a formal line of march. Supervision is to oversee or direct. Succession is one after another. Confusion means to be mixed up. Suspension is to stop or cease for a while. A wedding is a happy occasion. A funeral is a sad occasion.

In the speech on the occasion of his seventieth birthday, Professor Mason used Lincoln's expression, "Four score and seven years ago." Professor Mason is a medical man by profession. As a birthday gift, he asked for permission to make an extension to the clinic. "Expansion is needed to take care of all the patients." An extension is an increase in size. Expansion is an addition to the old.

# LESSON 77

**Soft g** - like **j** (g's name sound)
(when followed by **e, i,** or **y**)

After **soft g, e** is sounded in **-es**

**ge**

| age | edge | bilge | plunges |
| cage | badge | George | barges |
| page | budge | gorge | forges |
| rage | bulge | germ | urges |
| sage | dodge | hinge | large |
| wage | hedge | gem | fudge |
| huge | lodge | nudge | tinge |
| judge | bridge | wedge | fringes |
| grudge | drudge | singe | stages |
| pledge | trudge | sledge | lunge |
| dirge | scourge | smudge | ledges |

Words ending in **ge** followed by
a single consonant which is part of root word.
(If short vowel before soft **g** sound,
insert **d** before **g**.)

| fidget | badger | cudgel | budget | ledger |
| codger | gadget | smidgen | widget | midget |

**ange** as **ainge**

| angel | danger | strange | arrange | deranged |
| change | dangerous | stranger | grange | ranger |
| ranges | exchange | estrange | mange | manger |
| changeable | interchange | endanger | disarrange | arrangement |

*Exceptions:* orange   angelic

## LESSON 77—(Continued)

> In more-than-one-syllable words ending in **ge**, the vowel before **ge** can be either long or short.

| Long vowel before ge | Short vowel before ge | | | |
|---|---|---|---|---|
| engage | image | cottage | average | garbage |
| rampage | damage | visage | vintage | allege |
| refuge | savage | courage | village | forage |
| refugee | usage | vantage | pillage | encourage |
| deluge | bandage | advantage | steerage | suffrage |
| centrifuge | mucilage | storage | cartage | coverage |
| oblige | college | manage | cartilage | umbrage |
| enrage | | | | |
| subterfuge | | | | |

> Soft **g** as **zh**

| | | |
|---|---|---|
| collage | garage | corsage |
| mirage | montage | barrage |
| | massage | |

> Retaining **e** after **soft g** when next letter is not **i** or **y**

| | | | |
|---|---|---|---|
| surgeon | advantageous | chargeable | savagely |
| sturgeon | courageous | salvageable | savageness |
| bludgeon | encouragement | management | savagery |
| gorgeous | engagement | manageable | imagery |
| umbrageous | pigeon | pageant | pageantry |

## LESSON 77—(Continued)

## DRILL

| | | | |
|---|---|---|---|
| legend | bandages | damaged | revenge |
| images | congested | largest | impinge |
| indulge | regent | larger | ingestion |
| gentle | savages | cottages | digestion |
| gently | judges | pledged | indigestion |
| Gentile | oranges | indigent | congestion |
| gender | colleges | indigenous | suffragette |
| German | manager | challenge | peerage |
| regency | partridge | porridge | cartridge |

*Non-Phonic:*   *mortgage  gauge  margarine*
                  *marriage  carriage  sergeant*

## LESSON 78

**Soft g** - same sound as **j**
(when followed by **e, i,** or **y**)

**gi**

| | | | |
|---|---|---|---|
| digit | giant | margin | aging |
| ginger | frigid | giraffe | changing |
| origin | imagine | engineer | lodging |
| regiment | legislate | legitimate | judging |
| engine | gigantic | surgical | pledging |
| magic | magician | lethargic | incorrigible |
| region | legion | religion | collegiate |

163

## LESSON 78—(Continued)

**gy**

| | | | |
|---|---|---|---|
| clergy | dingy | orgy | Gypsy |
| apology | stingy | effigy | prodigy |
| spongy | geology | theology | gymnastics |
| energy | gypsum | gym | Egypt |
| gypped | lethargy | anthology | analogy |
| doxology | mythology | dermatology | criminology |

| gg has hard sound | | Hard and Soft C (See Lesson 72) | |
|---|---|---|---|
| beg-ging | soggy | critic | accuse |
| ragged | drugget | critical | accident |
| foggy | muggy | criticize | accord |
| bigger | sluggish | criticism | occur |
| bragger | trigger | cynical | accede |
| clogged | chigger | cynicism | occult |
| druggist | jigger | electrical | accelerate |
| dagger | sagging | electricity | election |
| nugget | rugged | accept | streptococcus |
| chugging | baggy | facetious | decelerate |

*Non-Phonic: suggest exaggerate*

| Root Words | | Suffixed Words | | |
|---|---|---|---|---|
| Examples of hard g followed by e, i, or y | | Hard g remains hard even when followed by e, i, or y | | |
| gig | finger | long-est | bringing | longing |
| give | linger | singing | younger | longish |
| get | anger | hanger | ringing | banged |
| gear | gift | stringy | clinging | tangy |
| giggle | gynecology | stronger | swinging | youngish |

164

# LESSON 78—(Continued)

## EXERCISES

"Don't cross the bridge until you get to it." "Don't change horses in the middle of the stream." A place of higher learning is called a college. In a circus, the wild animals are kept in cages. A giraffe is a gentle, long-necked animal.

A city dude spent his summer vacation in a village. One day he came to the general store itching to have some fun with the manager. He asked the manager if he had any gas ranges for sale. The man, busily engaged in arranging his stock on the shelves, answered with a short "No." "Surely you must sell large sized barges?" From this second inquiry, the old man was quick to judge what the dude was up to, so he said, "No, no barges. We sold the last one to Noah." The young smarty Aleck, enraged that he was not successful in getting the villager angry, said, "Just to change the subject, I notice that your ears are very large for a man your size." "Yes," answered the man gently, "you are right. For a man my size, my ears are very large, but for a donkey your age, your ears are very small."

George Washington was a great general. He feared no danger; he dodged no duty. With the intelligence of a sage and the gentility of an angel, with diligence and energy, he led his regiments to victory and won for us everlasting freedom. We pledge allegiance to his flag, the red, white, and blue, forever.

A digit is any one of the ten numerals. There are seven digits to a million. A finger or toe is also a digit. Some people are stingy; others are generous. These pages are legible. They are in clear print on fine paper and easy on the eyes to read. Ginger ale is a beverage with a pungent taste. We get ginger from a certain spicy plant. A beverage is a drink, and pungent means stinging or biting.

# LESSON 79

**tu as chu**
(Long u construction)
(Not in first syllable of root word)

| | | | |
|---|---|---|---|
| nature | fixture | rapture | furniture |
| pasture | vulture | virtue | literature |
| feature | capture | gesture | adventure |
| mixture | culture | actual | century |
| venture | creature | sculpture | virtuous |
| posture | puncture | scripture | punctual |
| torture | rupture | structure | natural |
| picture | saturate | spatula | cultural |
| statue | impetuous | ritual | accentuate |
| actuary | statute | statutory | virtuoso |
| punctuate | mortuary | perpetual | actuality |
| statuette | eventuality | capitulate | Gargantua |
| actuarial | saturation | fortunate | petulance |
| fortune | situation | tarantula | sanctuary |
| statuary | fluctuate | petulant | tortuous |

## EXERCISES

One hundred years is a century. We live in the twentieth century. The Bible is called "Holy Scriptures." The Holy Scriptures is the best literature in the world. Literature is high quality reading matter. Not everything printed is literature. Every home is furnished with some kind of furniture. Tables, beds, and chairs are furniture. Curtain rods, pictures, and refrigerators are fixtures. An electrical lamp is also a fixture.

Temperature is the degree of heat. High temperature means very hot. The patient has a high temperature means the sick person has a high fever. A vulture is a large bird. A vulture eats living or dead

## LESSON 79—(Continued)

animals or birds. Nature is the best healer. Medicine is a mixture of two, three, or more ingredients. Mixture is several things mixed together. Nature paints the hills and forests with a mixture of natural colors. Anything real, not artificial, is natural.

The cattle graze in the green pastures. A pasture is a grassy land where horses and cattle graze. Be kind to all animals. Do not torture them. To torture any living creature is a crime. To torture is to inflict pain; to hurt. To be kind and merciful is a great virtue. Only those who are virtuous are really great.

We admire George Washington for his virtue and culture, which were engraved in every feature of his face. Culture is refinement and education. "Nothing ventured, nothing gained" means if you do not dare or risk, you cannot expect to win.

## LESSON 80

| ei as long a | eigh as long a (ei as long a, gh silent) | | ey as long a |
|---|---|---|---|
| weigh | eight | freight | weighs |
| sleigh | weighed | weighty | eighty |
| weight | eighteen | neighbor | weighing |
| neigh | weightless | eightieth | freighter |
| | | | |
| their | rein | veil | reindeer |
| vein | beige | reinless | heinous |
| skein | seine | lei | surveillance |
| | | | |
| they | whey | purvey | survey |
| hey | grey | convey | obey |
| prey | bey | abeyance | conveyance |

*Exceptions:* *height* *sleight*

## LESSON 80—(Continued)
## EXERCISES

There is only one sure way to weigh a thing, put it on a scale. He who is not lazy and does not wait to be reminded is worth his weight in gold. I ate breakfast at eight o'clock. Ate means did eat, and eight is the number after seven. A horse neighs. Carat is weight. My ring is eighteen carat gold. Diamonds are sold by carats.

A sleigh is a vehicle on runners, not on wheels. In the winter we go sleigh riding. To slay is to kill. My teacher, Mrs. Creighton, does not seem to remember her times table. Yesterday she told us that eight times ten makes eighty, and today she said that ten times eight makes eighty. Ten and eight is eighteen. Eight and ten is also eighteen. My grandfather's eightieth birthday was last week.

In a fight, both fighters are in the same height and weight category; heavyweights or lightweights. Some people are overweight; others are underweight. My neighbor, Mr. Bright, used to be a heavyweight prize fighter. Mr. Bright is a neighborly neighbor. He is rarely home. He is an engineer on a freight train. Sometimes a freight train has as many as eighty-eight freight cars pulled by one engine. A passenger train travels faster than a freight train.

## LESSON 81

### ei and ie as ee

| ei after c, cei | ie after other consonants |||
| --- | --- | --- | --- |
| ceiling | yield | belief | pier |
| conceit | field | believe | wield |
| conceive | fierce | thief | brief |
| conceivable | piece | thieves | grievance |
| deceive | priest | relief | grievous |
| perceive | shield | relieve | cavalier |
| receive | shriek | grief | mien |
| receiver | pierce | grieve | tier |
| deceit | fiend | achieve | cashier |
| deceitful | retrieve | chief | reprieve |

## LESSON 81—(Continued)

<u>ei or ie after s</u>

seize    siege
seizure   besiege

*Exceptions:* *either  neither  leisure  weird  sheik*
*Non-Phonic:* *soldier  receipt  friend  sieve  forfeit*

## EXERCISES

When two people quarrel, the one who yields and ceases first is the wiser. "A friend in need is a friend indeed." "One true friend is worth a hundred kin." Keep your friendship in constant repair.

The son of a wealthy merchant had his picture painted by an artist. Many months had passed, and the painter did not receive any payment. In the belief that it was due to oversight, he went to see the merchant as a gentle reminder. The merchant was very happy to meet the artist and told him that the picture was a masterpiece, a fine piece of art. "You have achieved great success. Every feature in it is just like my son." The artist, seizing this opportunity, said, "I am glad that you like it, but I'm sorry to say that your son has not paid for it yet." "To my great grief," answered the father, "that also is just like my son."

Those who serve in the navy are called sailors and those who serve Uncle Sam in the army are called soldiers. The sailors and soldiers are the armed forces that protect us on land and sea.

A thief broke into Mrs. Priest's home and stole her ring, which had a stone in it weighing two carats. Mrs. Priest's shrieks pierced the air when she discovered the robbery. She was grieved by the loss of her lovely ring, but she was relieved that the thief had not stolen more of her prized possessions.

## LESSON 81—(Continued)

The police will seize the thieves. The judge will sentence the deceitful burglars, and they shall pay for the grief they have inflicted upon so many citizens.

Mr. Shields painted the ceiling in his kitchen. When he completed the job, he ate a large piece of steak, which gave him indigestion. He drank some hot tea in the belief that it would relieve his pain. Mr. Pierce has a farm. If his wheat field yields more bushels of grain than it did last year, he will receive sufficient money to buy some necessary equipment. He hopes that he can achieve his goal this season.

## LESSON 82

> **y** preceded by consonant
> changed to **i** when suffix is added

### READ ACROSS

| | | |
|---|---|---|
| happy | - | happier, happiest, happily, happiness |
| duty | - | duties, dutiable, dutiful, dutifully, dutifulness |
| study | - | studied, studies, studious, studiously, studiousness |
| worry | - | worries, worried, worrier, worriedly |

> One-syllable root words
> Change **y** to **i**
> generally, only when adding **-ed, -er, -es,** and **-est**

### READ ACROSS

| | | |
|---|---|---|
| dry | - | dries, dried, driest, drier (also dryer) |
| shy | - | shies, shied, shier (also shyer), shiest (also shyest) |

## LESSON 82—(Continued)

**y not changed to i when vowel precedes y**

### READ ACROSS

| | | |
|---|---|---|
| convey | - | conveys, conveyed, conveyance, conveyer (also conveyor) |
| play | - | plays, played, player, playful |
| buy | - | buys, buyer |
| guy | - | guys, guyed |
| pay | - | pays, payment, payable, paymaster, paycheck, payload, payoff, payroll, payer (or payor), payee |

*Non-Phonic:* daily

**y not changed to i when adding suffix beginning with i**

### READ ACROSS

| | | |
|---|---|---|
| lobby | - | lobbying, lobbyist, lobbyism |
| baby | - | babying, babyish |

### DRILL

| | | | |
|---|---|---|---|
| attorneys | journeyed | mightiest | slyness |
| groceries | dirtied | journeyman | wealthiest |
| journeying | ladies | earlier | melodies |
| thirtyish | shyly | graying | scurrying |
| fairies | fancied | laziest | hurried |
| grayish | luckiest | carried | parties |
| livelier | pennies | easier | **funniest** |
| daisies | heavier | families | **married** |
| pitied | buried | tarried | copyist |

# LESSON 83

**Verbs** ending in
- - **fy**     - - **ly**
(**y long**)

| - - fy | | - - ly | |
|---|---|---|---|
| notify | qualify | ally | comply |
| justify | pacify | rely | supply |
| modify | purify | apply | multiply |
| signify | specify | reply | imply |

*Exceptions:* July  occupy  deny  lullaby  bully

**Long y** changed to **long i** when suffix is added

| | | | |
|---|---|---|---|
| verifier | typifies | denial | appliance |
| mystifies | identifiable | satisfies | supplier |
| defied | unified | certified | occupies |
| defiant | compliance | relies | terrified |
| testified | simplified | sanctified | pacifier |
| reliance | allies | justifiable | glorifies |
| reliable | alliance | gratifies | multiplier |

**Long y** changed to **short i** when suffix is added
(mainly -**cation**)

| | | | |
|---|---|---|---|
| application | intensification | qualification | certificate |
| implication | amplification | modification | multiplicand |
| notification | ratification | nullification | multiplication |
| personification | solidification | electrification | identification |
| falsification | classification | fortification | purification |

172

# LESSON 83—(Continued)

## EXERCISES

The days are short and my duties are many. The lazier the person, the heavier his load. The happier you are, the easier your task. Take care of your pennies, and the dollars will take care of themselves. He who has strength is mighty, but he who can control himself is mightier. He who has much money is wealthy, but he who is contented with what he has is wealthier.

This is a lady's handbag. These are ladies' handbags. The ladies pick daisies for the babies. In a grocery store, groceries are sold. There are many kinds of berries. The hobbies of the heads of the three families on this block are varied. One studies, the second is always worrying with pets, and the third loves parties. Milton studied hard, then applied for the position and qualified. Today he occupies a high position and is satisfied.

A girl clerk in the office of a supplies store used to be tardy every day. One day the manager said to her, "Miss Jones, I notice that you come in late." Miss Jones quickly replied, "Yes, that is why I always leave earlier than the others."

Tommy was always tardy or absent from class and always had the funniest and snappiest excuses ready to offer. One day the teacher asked Tommy why he was absent on Monday. "I hurried and fell in the mud. I dirtied my face and went back home to wash it," he replied. "Well, and what happened Tuesday?" "I carried my lunch in a paper bag, and a dog snatched it from my hand, so I let him have my pencils and lessons also." "Why are you late today?" asked the teacher. "Your nose testifies that you were in a fight." "No, ma'am. I bit off my nose to spite my face." "But, Tommy, you can't reach your nose with your teeth." "I got up on a chair," was Tommy's quick answer.

# PART III

## Compound Vowels and Consonants
## Two Vowels Side by Side, Both Sounded
## Two Consonants Side by Side, One Silent
## Homonyms

---

## LESSON 84

### Long oo

| boot | booth | cool | coop |
| doom | boom | food | fool |
| mood | loot | loom | moon |
| noon | poor | pool | roof |
| root | room | soon | tool |
| tooth | moose | noose | loose |
| goose | soothe | shoot | choose |
| boost | booze | roost | ooze |
| brood | croon | droop | gloom |
| groom | groove | proof | smooth |
| snooze | spool | spoon | stool |
| stoop | troop | swoon | swoop |

### DRILL

| cooler | doomed | foolishly | moody |
| looted | poorly | roofer | rooted |
| roomers | sooner | shooting | chooses |
| booster | rooster | oozing | brooded |

## LESSON 84—(Continued)

| voodoo   | balloon    | igloo    | tycoon   |
|----------|------------|----------|----------|
| bamboo   | soothsayer | booty    | bootee   |
| crooner  | drooping   | gloomy   | scooped  |
| smoothly | snoozing   | spoonful | trooper  |
| cartoon  | platoon    | reproof  | taboo    |
| pontoon  | raccoon    | festoon  | cocoon   |

## EXERCISES

Once on a moonlit night, a fox, hungry for food, decided to loot the chicken coops on a nearby farm. He had a sweet tooth for a nice fat goose, but he said if the worst comes to the worst, a rooster will do. He soon reached the roost where all the roosters were peacefully snoozing. He stopped at the well in the middle of the yard and bent his head to see what was in there. The full moon reflected in the water of the well appeared to him as a big loaf of toothsome cheese.

The fox mused, "Everything goes smoothly so far. Why start with those fool roosters. They might wake up the neighbors. Cheese, too, is a very delicious food and safer to get." He noticed a wide bucket tied to the end of a rope hanging on a pulley in the well. The fox leaped into the empty bucket and hit the bottom of the well in a jiffy, while at the same time, the bucket tied to the other end of the rope went up.

The fox said, "The proof of the pudding is in eating it, and I am all set to eat." He smelled and stirred in the water. Well, sir, he had to admit that this time he fooled himself and fell into a trap. There was neither dinner nor a way of escape. Gloomy and with drooping head, he sat in the bucket brooding over his hard luck and awaiting his doom.

In the meantime, the wolf, starved as usual, came snooping for a bite on the same farm. The wolf ventured up to the well to take a peep. "Hi, buddy, is that you? I see you have a feast, and poor me, I have not had a spoonful to eat in three days. I wish you'd let me keep you company." "Why, sure," said the fox, "there is plenty of room here

## LESSON 84—(Continued)

for you, too. Just get into that bucket, and soon you will be treated to a nice, cool piece of cheese." The wolf did as he was told. The wolf's weight, being heavier than that of the fox, carried the wolf deep into the well while lifting the fox up. The fox, in a happy mood again, yelled to the wolf, "Thanks for the lift. Eat as much as you choose, buddy. I hope you have a pleasant time."

## LESSON 85

### Short oo

| hook    | foot   | booked   | motherhood   |
| ------- | ------ | -------- | ------------ |
| look    | soot   | booklet  | falsehood    |
| nook    | good   | brooklet | neighborhood |
| took    | hood   | crooked  | likelihood   |
| book    | wood   | hooded   | livelihood   |
| cook    | wool   | looking  | childhood    |
| brook   | wooden | cooked   | manhood      |
| crook   | woody  | goodness | womanhood    |
| shook   | woolen | football | brotherhood  |
| cookies | woolly | footrest | sisterhood   |

*Non-Phonic:* flood   blood   floor   door

### EXERCISES

### Real Charity

Many years ago, in the horse and buggy days, there lived a man who made his livelihood from repairing watches. He occupied one room in the poorer neighborhood of the small city. In one nook of his room, he had a desk which served as his workshop, and the rest he used as a bedroom and kitchen.

# LESSON 85—(Continued)

His furniture consisted of an iron bed, a small table and a chair, a large bookcase full of books, and a cook stove. In the daytime he attended to his poorly paying business. He did not need much. He was a bachelor, alone in the world. The early part of the night, he was seen reading or studying his good books, but late at night, so the rumor went, he'd disappear. A man in the neighborhood made up his mind to keep an eye on the watchmaker. The man reasoned that he must be a crook, or else he'd not leave late at night. So the man stood across the street to spy on the watchmaker's every move.

After midnight, he noticed the bachelor put on a short leather coat and tie it with a heavy rope. He stuck a hatchet under the rope, and with a woolen scarf at his neck, he left with hurried steps. He crossed the frozen brooklet, which bordered a thickly wooded forest. There he stopped, looked a while, then began chopping down a good sized tree. That done, he split the tree into logs, tied them into a large bundle, took the bundle on his back, and was off toward the city again.

He came to a shack and rapped on the door. Someone from the inside asked who it was. "Do you want to buy some wood?" the early caller asked. "Wood!" repeated the woman inside. "My dear man, I haven't the strength to get up from my bed to build a fire. I haven't cooked or eaten any warm food in three days." "I'll be glad to fix the fire for you," said the insistent salesman. "You see, I am very cold, too." "No," replied the woman, "I am sorry, but I have no money to buy the wood." "Don't let that worry you either," answered the man. "You'll pay me when you get well and able." "All right," said the woman, "if you insist, come in."

The next day the skeptic told of his adventure and remarked, "That man is a saint. What we need to do is not watch him, but help him in his noble work." May we have many of his type.

# LESSON 86

**au** **aw**

| 1 | 2 | 3 | 4 |
|---|---|---|---|
| haul | law | flaw | awning |
| Paul | jaw | claw | lawyer |
| pause | paw | slaw | awkward |
| cause | saw | draw | brawny |
| fault | raw | crawl | awful |
| haunt | bawl | shawl | daughter |
| fraud | dawn | brawl | naughty |
| launch | hawk | straw | August |
| gauze | lawn | pawn | because |
| aught | yawn | squawk | launder |
| caught | prawn | fawn | cautious |
| taught | brawn | craw | saucy |

## DRILL

| | | | |
|---|---|---|---|
| dawned | drawer | pawned | flawless |
| lawless | lawful | sawing | slaughter |
| laurel | laundry | laundress | crawling |
| haunted | faulty | faultless | auction |
| taunted | gaudy | hauling | causes |
| astronaut | cosmonaut | nausea | fraudulent |
| gawky | faucet | automatic | caution |
| jaundice | automobile | bylaws | authorities |
| applaud | caucus | automation | laundromat |

*Non-Phonic:* gauge

## LESSON 86—(Continued)

### EXERCISES

Where there is no law, there are no manners. Where there are no manners, there is no law. Your brother's wife is your sister-in-law. Your brothers' wives are your sisters-in-law. Your sister's husband is your brother-in-law. Your sisters' husbands are your brothers-in-law. My brother-in-law's name is Maurice.

A thing not cooked or baked is raw. Most people do not eat meat raw. The hawk tears its prey with its claws. The vulture has sharp claws. The jaw is a part of the face. The teeth are set in the jaw bones.

Straw is the stem of grain. Straw is of little value. In the summer we wear hats that are made of straw. Sliced cabbage with salad dressing is called cole slaw. Because you are not faultless yourself, don't find fault with others. There is nothing that is perfect or flawless; even the sun has flaws. Don't cast stones into the well from which you draw water.

An automobile is a car that goes automatically. That means it moves by itself. All one has to do is to operate the proper appliances. Astronauts from the United States have the distinction of being the first persons to land on the surface of the moon.

A wise woman told her daughter who was going to be married soon, "My daughter, if you will respect your husband like a king, he will treat you like a queen."

## LESSON 87

**ough as au**

| fought | bought | sought |
| ought | thought | brought |
|  | nought |  |

## LESSON 87—(Continued)

**Four words beginning with th and containing ough**
**(Different sounds of ough)**

| 1 | 2 | 3 | 4 |
|---|---|---|---|
| ough as long o | ough as au | ough as long oo | ough as either long o or schwa sound |
| though | thought | through | thorough |

## EXERCISES

We are taught to pause and stand respectfully while the U.S. flag passes by. Paul works in a laundry. He rises at dawn, and all day he hauls bundles to be laundered. At night Paul studies law. Soon he will be a good lawyer. His sister is a laundress.

August is the last month of the summer. Because the month of August is usually very hot, many people take their vacation in August. In a sawmill, logs are sawed into lumber. Wood is lumber.

Saw is the past tense of see. Caught is the past tense of catch. "Did you see my hack saw?" "Yes, I saw your daughter saw the bench on the lawn with your hack saw." A daughter is a female child. She is a naughty girl sometimes. I sought for my saw all over the place. Sought is seek in the past and means "looked for." Brought means "did bring." "Paul, did you buy the woolen shawl?" "Yes, I bought it yesterday."

It takes two to make a fight. When two people quarrel, the first one to cease is the smarter. The two friends fought side by side in the World War. "Ought for naught" means you can't get anything for nothing. "A penny for your thoughts" means "Tell me what you are thinking."

# LESSON 88

**ou**  **ow**

| our | bound | bow | towel |
| out | found | cow | tower |
| loud | pound | how | power |
| foul | cloud | now | shower |
| house | shout | down | flower |
| south | stout | gown | crowded |
| mouth | scout | crowd | drowned |
| mouse | count | brown | drowning |
| round | mount | frown | township |
| sound | shroud | town | frowning |
| hound | proud | crown | powerless |
| couch | scour | owl | flounder |
| flounce | vouch | drowse | coward |

## DRILL

| amount | mounted | mountain | ours |
| mountainous | ourselves | outward | stouter |
| mouthful | loudest | sounded | counted |
| soundly | cloudy | scouting | brownish |
| proudly | gowned | crowned | clown |
| household | housemaid | bounced | powerful |
| drowsy | flowery | allowance | dismounted |
| outrageous | pronounce | dowager | prowess |
| trowel | outlandish | prowler | denounce |

**ough as ou**

| bough | drought | plough | doughty |

*Non-Phonic:* *counterfeit*

# LESSON 88—(Continued)

## EXERCISES

There are sixteen ounces to a pound. A pound is a dry measure. To have sound teeth and a healthy mouth, brush your teeth and wash your mouth after you eat. "Don't count your chickens before they hatch." A chicken is a fowl. A town is smaller than a city and larger than a village. One powerhouse can supply several towns with electricity. Electricity is power. Some powerhouses have towers in which there is a town clock. It is quiet around a farmhouse at night. You can't hear a sound except that of the hound. A hound is a hunting dog.

"Out of sight, out of mind." When on a visit, the first day you are a guest, the second day you cause unrest, and on the third day you become a pest. April showers are good for plants and flowers. Ground grain is flour. From the flour we make bread. Wheat flour is white; rye flour is brown.

A very high and large hill is a mountain. Some mountains are so high they reach the clouds. A very heavy downpour of rain is sometimes called a "cloudburst." In some cities there are mounted police. Policemen who do duty on horseback are mounted police. A great number of people in one place is a crowd. At certain times of the day, the streets in the downtown business area are very crowded.

To shout is to yell. A shout is a very loud cry. A shower is a local rain of short duration. Do not judge by outward appearance; you may be fooled. A gown is a woman's dress. An evening gown is a fancy dress worn at dances, parties, or weddings. The funny man in a circus is a clown.

A man who saw a dead body floating on the surface of the water said, "What a pity! You were drowned because you caused the boat to tilt." To feel drowsy is to be very sleepy. Some people sleep soundly. They don't wake easily. A king is a crowned ruler. A crown is an ornament on a king's head.

## LESSON 89

**ou**    **ow**

**(like o long)**

| | | | |
|---|---|---|---|
| owe | flow | hallow | widowed |
| low | glow | hollow | growers |
| tow | throw | yellow | slowly |
| row | below | borrow | soul |
| show | bellow | window | soulless |
| crow | willow | swallow | flowing |
| blow | wallow | grown | owners |
| slow | fellow | towed | slowest |
| snow | mellow | rowing | lower |
| grow | billow | showed | yellowish |
| poultry | pillow | borrowed | elbow |
| shoulder | boulder | poultice | cantaloupe |
| shouldering | soulful | poultices | poultryman |

**ough as long o**

dough     though     thorough     furlough     although
borough

**NINE SOUNDS OF OU**

**1. ou as in *out***
**(See Lesson 88.)**

| | | | | |
|---|---|---|---|---|
| pouch | flounder | announce | devout | account |
| carouse | gouge | encounter | flout | ounce |

183

## LESSON 89—(Continued)

### 2. ou as long o

| souls | poultry | boulders |
| shouldered | coulter | cantaloupes |

### 3. ou as long oo
### (See Lesson 65.)

| soup | route | group | croup | rouge |
| acoustics | crouton | souvenir | nougat | roulette |
| wound | bouffant | cougar | routine | louver |

### 4. ou as short oo

boulevard

(See Lesson 99:   could   should   would)

### 5. ou as aw
### (See Lesson 87.)

| bought | nought | thought | sought | brought |

### 6. ou as short u

*(accented)*

| touch | touchdown | country | double | cousin |
| couple | coupling | southern | trouble | untroubled |

(See Lesson 93:   tough   rough   enough)

# LESSON 89—(Continued)

*(unaccented)*

| | | | | |
|---|---|---|---|---|
| enormous | grievous | delicious | tremendous | fabulous |
| | camouflage | carousel | anxiously | |

### 7. our as er
### (See Lesson 62.)

| | | | |
|---|---|---|---|
| journals | scourge | encourage | flourishing |
| nourishes | courtesy | glamour | journeys |

### 8. our as short oor

| | | | | |
|---|---|---|---|---|
| tour | tourist | velour | courier | tournament |

### 9. our as or
### (See Lesson 61.)

| | | | | |
|---|---|---|---|---|
| yourself | fourteenth | courtyard | mournful | pouring |
| source | gourd | fourth | courses | resource |

## EXERCISES

Man sees a mote in his neighbor's eye, but cannot see a beam in his own eye. Judge not your fellowman until you have been placed in his position. "People who live in glass houses should not throw stones." A widow is a woman who has lost her husband by death. A widower is a man who lost his wife by death. Mrs. Brown is a widow. Mr. Trout is a widower.

Mr. Brown is an apple grower. He has three grown sons. Mrs. Brown has a dairy farm with many milking cows. She was left a widow

## LESSON 89—(Continued)

with three beautiful grown daughters. It is better to go to bed without supper than to borrow and owe. If you must borrow, pay back what you owe on time. What you borrow is not your own. You owe that to the other fellow. We don't always own the house in which we live. We pay rent to the owner for the use of it.

An elbow is a part of the body. The elbow is the bend in the arm. It is a rude fellow who elbows his way through a crowd. You may follow the crowd, but you don't elbow through it. Low is the opposite of high. In the North, the temperature is lower than down South. The higher we go the lower the temperature.

Below is the opposite of above. To be content, look below you. To be wise, look above you. Below means underneath or lower down. To bellow is to roar. The hollow, loud cry of a bull or cow is a roar. The difference between below and bellow is one "L." A bellows is a wind bag; an instrument with which the blacksmith blows the fire to make the iron glow quicker.

A great wave of the sea is called a billow—the billows of the ocean. The water of the rivers flows into the sea. The ocean is not a flowing body of water. When the snow melts, the water flows into the brooks and rivers, which makes them swell, and the water gets yellowish.

## LESSON 90

**oi**  **oy**

| oil | point | boiler | poison |
| boil | joint | coined | rejoice |
| coil | hoist | toiler | pointer |
| coin | moist | foiled | spoiled |
| join | poise | noisy | coinage |
| soil | spoil | loiter | hoister |
| toil | broil | adjoin | ointment |

## LESSON 90—(Continued)

| void | joist | rejoin | appointment |
| loin | foist | broiler | poisonous |
| noise | avoid | appoint | noiseless |
| foil | exploit | doily | embroider |
| broil | parboil | thyroid | equipoise |

| boy | loyal | loyalty | employer |
| joy | royal | royalty | employee |
| toy | oyster | joyous | employment |
| enjoy | employ | boyish | enjoyment |
| annoy | destroy | coyly | boyhood |
| decoy | joyful | annoyed | destroyer |
| alloy | voyage | flamboyant | annoyance |
| soybean | boycott | gargoyle | envoy |
| deploy | convoy | corduroy | deployment |

*Non-Phonic:* porpoise   tortoise   poignant   buoy   coyote

## EXERCISES

A penny, a nickel, a dime, a quarter, and a silver dollar are coins. A toy is a plaything. To avoid trouble, don't get into it. Water boiled and cooled is safer to drink than if it is not boiled. A hot water tank is a boiler. The water in the boiler gets hot from a coil which is heated. A coil is a pipe wound round and round like a snake. To enjoy life, avoid trouble. The joys of life are many. To feel well and to be able to work is a joy. Some people enjoy reading good books, others enjoy open air sports, and still others enjoy a good motion picture show. A coin or two in an empty jug makes a lot of noise.

A boy is a male child. The boy grows into manhood; the girl grows into womanhood. When the boy is full grown, he must find

## LESSON 90—(Continued)

some employment. Employment is a profession, occupation, or work. The one who gives employment is the employer, and the one who is employed by another is an employee. A boil is an inflamed sore. For every boil there is an ointment. Ointment is a soothing oil. Oil is a fatty, greasy liquid. Oil is used for many things, as a lubricant or motor oil. We use oil in cooking foods, for frying, and for baking.

An oyster is a seafood. The oyster season begins in about September. We prepare and eat oysters in several styles. Oysters are eaten in the months that have an "r" in them.

## LESSON 91

eu    ew

Long u sounds

| few | grew | threw | brewery |
| dew | stew | screw | jewel |
| hew | slew | shrewd | jewelry |
| pew | drew | sinew | anew |
| new | blew | pewter | renew |
| news | crew | newly | curfew |
| brew | flew | fewer | stewed |

| feud | Europe | neuter | deuce |
| neutral | Teutonic | eulogy | neutrality |
| euthanasia | neuritis | sleuth | Beulah |
| feudal | aneurysm | neurology | eucalyptus |
| Eurasian | Deuteronomy | Zeus | leucocyte |

*Non-Phonic:*  view   review   sew   lieu   lieutenant

## LESSON 91—(Continued)

### EXERCISES

A new broom sweeps clean. New is the opposite of old. Few persons see their own faults. Truth is heavy. That is why so few carry it.

How do animals speak?

The dog barks, "I watch the house."
The cat mews, "I catch the mouse."
The hen cackles, "I lay eggs for you."
The swine grunts, "I give you ham and bacon to chew."
The horse neighs, "I carry you and pull the load, too."
The cow moos, "I give you milk, butter, and meat to stew."
The rooster crows, "I wake you when the sun comes into view."
The sheep bleats, "My wool keeps you warm and grows anew."

A pew is a seat in a church. In a church or house of worship people sit in pews. Pewter is a metal. Pewter does not shine as brightly as silver. Yale University is in New Haven, Connecticut. New Haven is a city in a New England state. New York, New York, and Tokyo, Japan, are the largest cities in the world. California and New York are the most populated states in this country. For newsy news, we read the daily newspapers.

Andrew was a mischievous boy. While the teacher in Sunday school reviewed anew the story of Cain and Abel for the fourth time, Andrew grew restless. Instead of taking notes, he drew a few funny pictures in his notebook, then tore them into bits and strewed the pieces on the floor, or blew them into his neighbor's ears. He even unscrewed his seat and threw the screws around the room. One screw flew straight toward the teacher's head. The teacher turned to Andrew angrily and asked, "Andrew, who slew Abel?" Andrew drew up his shoulders and said, "Not me. I wasn't even near him."

# LESSON 92

> **TWO VOWELS SIDE BY SIDE, BOTH SOUNDED**

> Long vowel digraph — only first vowel sounded
> Long vowel digraph backwards — both vowels sounded

### ai - ia

| | | |
|---|---|---|
| plaint | - | pliant |
| train | - | triangle |
| vain | - | via |
| dairy | - | diameter |
| faint | - | defiance |
| rail | - | material |
| paid | - | Olympiad |
| brain | - | inebriated |
| avail | - | variation |
| rain | - | proletarian |
| saint | - | appreciate |
| pail | - | sepia |
| daisy | - | radiator |
| trail | - | memorial |
| gain | - | giant |
| stain | - | enthusiasm |

### ui - iu

| | | |
|---|---|---|
| nuisance | - | genius |
| fruit | - | stadium |
| suit | - | diuretic |
| cruise | - | radius |
| bruise | - | auditorium |
| juice | - | diurnal |
| recruit | - | medium |
| pursuit | - | magnesium |
| sluice | - | calcium |
| suitor | - | aquarium |
| juicy | - | gymnasium |
| bruit | - | equilibrium |
| fruitful | - | symposium |
| Muir | - | premium |
| suitable | - | solarium |
| fruitless | - | wickiup |

### oa - ao

| | | |
|---|---|---|
| road | - | aorta |
| coast | - | chaos |
| loan | - | Laotian |
| moan | - | Naomi |

### oe - eo

| | | |
|---|---|---|
| Monroe | - | rodeo |
| toe | - | meteor |
| doe | - | video |
| foe | - | leotard |
| hoe | - | geometry |
| Joe | - | Leo |

## LESSON 92—(Continued)

| ay - ya | | |
|---|---|---|
| relay | - | polyandry |
| dismay | - | myasthenia |
| clay | - | kyack |
| dray | - | dryad |
| may | - | myalgia |
| say | - | cyanide |
| decay | - | kyanite |
| essay | - | cyanosis |
| way | - | wyandotte |
| portray | - | cyanotic |
| betray | - | cyanogenesis |

| oe - eo | | |
|---|---|---|
| Poe | - | ideology |
| roe | - | oleomargarine |
| woe | - | geology |
| oboe | - | courteous |
| throe | - | cameo |
| floe | - | neon |
| tiptoe | - | preoccupied |
| hoeing | - | stereo |
| toenail | - | preordained |
| woeful | - | meow |
| toehold | - | neologism |
| doeskin | - | leonine |

*Non-Phonic: people   leopard   jeopardy   yeoman   kayak*

> Compound vowels and diphthongs backwards
> Both vowels sounded

| au - ua | | |
|---|---|---|
| astronaut | - | issuable |
| plaudits | - | graduation |
| cause | - | casual |
| authority | - | truant |
| laurel | - | insinuation |
| bauble | - | pursuant |

| oi - io | | |
|---|---|---|
| boisterous | - | cardiogram |
| rejoice | - | riot |
| spoil | - | espionage |
| appoint | - | audio |
| noise | - | antibiotic |
| exploit | - | pioneer |

## LESSON 92—(Continued)

| au - ua | | | oi - io | | |
|---|---|---|---|---|---|
| nausea | - | eventuality | avoid | - | radio |
| plausible | - | perpetuate | sirloin | - | lion |
| auditor | - | issuance | foible | - | serious |
| maudlin | - | mutual | colloid | - | biopsy |
| faucet | - | actuary | embroider | - | seniority |
| Paul | - | Stuart | purloin | - | oblivion |
| daub | - | dual | parboil | - | ratio |
| saucy | - | continuation | voice | - | violent |
| haunt | - | usual | devoid | - | interior |
| vault | - | visual | joist | - | axiom |
| gauze | - | accentuate | moisture | - | sociology |
| autocrat | - | annual | cloister | - | iota |

| ou - uo | | | oy - yo | | |
|---|---|---|---|---|---|
| county | - | conspicuous | employ | - | embryo |
| devour | - | duo | decoy | - | Wyoming |
| poundage | - | ingenuous | boy | - | myopia |
| ounce | - | virtuoso | toy | - | cryogen |
| mousy | - | continuous | joy | - | bryology |
| thousand | - | innocuous | annoy | - | lyonnaise |
| dour | - | duopoly | enjoy | - | pyoderma |
| about | - | contemptuous | destroy | - | myocardium |
| founder | - | virtuosity | oysters | - | tryout |
| astound | - | contiguous | boycott | - | pyogenic |
| douse | - | duodenum | envoy | - | flyover |
| bounty | - | virtuous | loyalty | - | hyoid |

## LESSON 92—(Continued)

> Long vowel digraph at end of root word,
> only first vowel sounded
>
> When not at end of root word,
> both vowels sounded

| oe | | ue | | ye | |
|---|---|---|---|---|---|
| toe | - coefficient | true | - influence | lye | - polyester |
| Moe | - poem | blue | - bluet | rye | - hyena |
| sloe | - poetry | glue | - minuend | dye | - myelitis |
| | coed | | duel | | pyemia |
| | whoever | | influenza | | syenite |
| | coerce | | duet | | pyelitis |
| | Joel | | affluent | | |
| | coeditor | | puerile | | |
| | whomsoever | | innuendo | | |
| | coexecutor | | gruelling | | |
| | Noel | | cruel | | |
| | coexist | | fluency | | |
| | coeducational | | fuel | | |
| | coequal | | suet | | |

> - - iac (short **a**, but **k** is dropped from **ck** digraph)

| cardiac | zodiac | pyromaniac |
| sacroiliac | maniac | kleptomaniac |
| | dipsomaniac | |

## LESSON 92—(Continued)

**Examples of diphthong, compound, or long vowel combinations in which both vowels are sounded**

| ai | ui | ie | oa |
|---|---|---|---|
| dais | ruin | piety | boa |
| naive | bruin | lenient | oasis |
| mosaic | fruition | expedient | coalition |
| prosaic | tuition | society | Noah |
|  | annuity | variety | coaxial |
| **ea** | fluid | proprietor |  |
| reassure | suicide | notoriety | **ei** |
| preamble | intuition | diet | albeit |
| rearm | continuity | quiet | preignition |
| theater | ingenuity | science | reimburse |
| cereal | truism | nutrient | preinduction |
| althea |  | audience | reincarnation |
| meander | **oi** | biennium | deification |
|  |  | biennial |  |
| **eu** | sacroiliac | triennium | **oo** |
|  | stoic | multiethnic |  |
| museum | coincide | obedience | cooperation |
| peritoneum | coincidence | quietus | coordinate |
|  | heroism | sobriety |  |

## EXERCISES

Naomi plays the piano and Brian fiddles on the violin. Mrs. Marriott is usually very lenient. She told the children to turn down the radio and to be quiet, and they were genuinely cooperative. Manuel decided to read a book of poetry by his favorite poet, and Julius trimmed the thick foliage on the front lawn.

# LESSON 92—(Continued)

If it rains tomorrow, it will ruin the annual picnic sponsored by the Iota Society. Dr. Adrian Wyandotte diagnosed the ailment as a cardiac murmur. Vivian was overweight, but she has lost thirty pounds since she has been on her diet. She looks wonderful now and says the diet enables her to eat a variety of nourishing foods. In traveling throughout the United States, one hears many different dialects. Samuel kept copious notes in his diary, and the data enabled him to draw an excellent diagram of the viaduct.

Prior to the fourth period of the football game, the television cable broke, and we lost the audio and video portions of the program. Mr. Lawrence Ezekiel was supposed to officiate at the game, but an attack of influenza prevented him from attending, and he was conspicuous by his absence.

When the pioneers moved westward, they encountered numerous hazards. It was a continuous struggle to survive, and many men made heroic efforts to save the group. Henrietta read in her textbook on ancient history that the first one-way streets and off-street parking facilities were introduced in imperial Rome to keep chariot traffic moving smoothly. She also read that the wheel span of the Roman chariots was exactly equal to today's standard gauge railroad tracks.

Among the interesting items in the scrapbook of information that Joel compiled are the following entries: Identifying numerals weren't used on football jerseys until almost 40 years after the first intercollegiate contest. About 120 years B.C., Hero of Alexandria became the father of automation when he invented the aeolipile, a turbine engine that opened the temple doors. Scientists have found that all bears in Yellowstone National Park enter their dens for winter sleep on the very same day. The world's largest crystal ball weighs 106 pounds, was carved in China, polished in Japan, and is now in the National Museum in Washington, D.C. A diamond's weight originally was figured against tiny carob tree seeds, which developed into the carat. Rice paper is made from a small Asiatic tree, not from rice.

# REVIEW

## Long Vowels

### Read Across

|  |  |  |  |  |
|---|---|---|---|---|
| ai | - | aim | train | strain |
| - - ay | - | lay | stay | spray |
| ee | - | see | feel | speed |
| ea | - | tea | clean | stream |
| oa | - | oats | road | float |

## Compound Vowels

### Read Across

|  |  |  |  |  |
|---|---|---|---|---|
| ea | - | head | ready | steady |
| oo | - | food | root | spoon |
| oo | - | cook | book | brook |
| au | - | Paul | fault | laundry |
| aw | - | saw | claw | straw |
| ou | - | out | round | proud |
| ow | - | now | down | brown |
| ou | - | soul | shoulder | poultry |
| ow | - | low | grow | fellow |
| oi | - | oil | join | broiler |
| oy | - | boy | destroy | enjoy |
| eu | - | feud | sleuth | neutral |
| ew | - | few | grew | pewter |

# LESSON 93

**gh as f**

| laugh | tough | rough | cough |
| trough | enough | laughed | laughing |
| laughter | tougher | toughest | roughly |
| rougher | roughest | coughed | coughing |
| slough | toughen | roughage | toughness |

draught (variation of *draft*)   hiccough (variation of *hiccup*)

## EXERCISES

"Laugh and the world laughs with you. Cry, and you cry alone." Enough is plenty. Cover your cough. Cough into your handkerchief. Wash your hands carefully whenever they come in contact with germs. Do not infect others. Do not neglect your cough. Get a good cough syrup. If that does not help, see a doctor.

Work toughens the muscles. Outdoor exercise toughens the body. The meat of a rooster is tougher than the meat of a hen. Horses and cows eat and drink from troughs. The baker mixes the dough in a trough. A trough is a long hollow receptacle.

Anything rough is not smooth. Wood, sawed but not planed, is rough. Uncivil, unrefined fellows are rough fellows. Some people look outwardly rough, yet are very tender at heart. That is why we say, "Do not judge by looks." It may be a diamond in the rough or a poisonous snake in the silky grass. Some people get along with what they have; others never have enough. A person may eat enough and sleep enough, but seldom does enough good. A good soldier is made tough, looks rough, and laughs in the face of danger.

# LESSON 94

**ph as f**

| | | |
|---|---|---|
| cipher | pharmacy | paragraph |
| orphan | physics | photograph |
| prophet | prophecy | phonograph |
| Philip | prophesy | physician |
| Joseph | asphalt | Philadelphia |
| Sophie | alphabet | stenography |
| nephew | sulphur | camphor |
| phrase | trophy | pamphlet |
| Murphy | triumph | photographer |
| sphere | telephone | stenographer |
| elephant | telegraph | photography |
| phantom | zephyr | emphasis |
| sphynx | emphysema | claustrophobia |
| dolphin | sophomore | pharmaceutical |
| lymph | philosophy | saxophone |
| typhoon | aphasia | hydrophobia |
| gopher | phosphate | symphony |

*Non-Phonic: catastrophe   apostrophe*

## EXERCISES

Your sister's or brother's son is your nephew. Your sister's or brother's daughters are your nieces. My sister's boy Joseph is my nephew. He calls me uncle. Mrs. Murphy and Mrs. Phillips are sisters. Mrs. Murphy's sons are Mrs. Phillips' nephews and Mrs. Phillips' daughters are Mrs. Murphy's nieces. Mrs. Phillips' children call Mrs. Murphy aunt and Mr. Murphy uncle. The children of Mrs. Murphy and Mrs. Phillips are cousins. Joseph and Philip and their sister Sophie are orphans. They are the children of the late Joseph Murphy, the pharmacist.

## LESSON 94—(Continued)

An orphan is a child who has lost his father or mother or both parents. We must be kind to orphans and widows. Poor orphans are taken care of in a home called an orphanage. A pharmacist is one who sells drugs and medicine. A pharmacy is a drugstore.

A prophet is one who foretells events. A prophet prophesies things to happen. The prophetic words of a seer are a prophecy. To prophesy is to foretell things to come in the future. A prophet prophesies a prophecy. A prophetess is a female prophet.

The letters from "a" to "z" in order are called the alphabet. A dictionary is arranged in alphabetical order. Cynthia read in a book of facts that the oldest letter is O, unchanged in shape since its adoption into the Phoenician alphabet between 1200 and 1300 B.C. She also read that in every herd of wild elephants, one takes the responsibility of frequently checking behind to be sure that all is well.

Philadelphia is the largest city in the state of Pennsylvania. Philadelphia is the birthplace of our "Declaration of Independence." The "Liberty Bell," which proclaimed our freedom to the world on July 4, 1776, is now housed in Independence Hall in Philadelphia.

An elephant is an African animal. The elephant is the largest animal in existence. A physician is a doctor of medicine. In case of sickness, call or see a physician. To telegraph is to send a message by wire. This message is called a telegram. To save time telegraph. A phonograph is an instrument reproducing the actual sound of the voice of a person or thing. A photograph is a picture. The photographer takes pictures by means of a photographic instrument with a lens. A photographic instrument with a lens is a camera. A telephone is one of the most useful things in a home. In case of fire, we telephone the fire department. In case of illness, we telephone for a physician. In case of trouble, we telephone the police.

# LESSON 95

### ch as k
### (Generally Greek-Latin origin)

| | | | |
|---|---|---|---|
| ache | stomach | chemist | architect |
| echo | chorus | schedule | chronicle |
| orchid | schooner | monarch | chemistry |
| school | broncho | orchestra | Christmas |
| scheme | scholar | technical | Christian |
| anchor | chronic | character | technician |
| chaos | matriarch | bronchitis | pulchritude |
| mechanic | chimera | zucchini | bronchial |
| chord | oligarchy | chameleon | cholesterol |
| trachea | chiropodist | strychnine | mechanism |
| chasm | dichotomy | anachronism | chronological |
| cholera | parochial | choreography | chiropractor |
| chrome | charisma | chlorine | catechism |

*Non-Phonic*   choir

### ch silent

| | | | |
|---|---|---|---|
| drachm | schism | yacht | fuchsia |

### ch as sh
### (Generally loan words from modern French or Spanish)

| | | | |
|---|---|---|---|
| chic | machine | chef | pistachio |
| chute | chagrin | chivalry | chaperon |
| fichu | chiffon | machete | charade |
| chaise | chauffeur | chalet | chandelier |
| cliche | attache | chicanery | touche |
| chateau | chapeau | parachute | charlatan |

200

## LESSON 95—(Continued)

| | | | |
|---|---|---|---|
| mustache | cache | chaparral | chauvinism |
| chevron | machinery | chartreuse | machinist |
| chanteuse | Charlotte | Chevrolet | chenille |
| sachet | brochure | ricochet | brochette |
| chiffonier | chifforobe | chantilly | parachutist |

### EXERCISES

A school is a place where we learn. Experience is the best school, but also the most costly. Children attending school are sometimes called scholars. Christmas is a Christian holiday. Christmas is a religious holiday which comes on the twenty-fifth of December. An architect is one who draws plans for buildings and bridges. The drawn plans of an architect are called "blue-prints."

A schedule is a timetable. Trains and airplanes run on scheduled time. A king, who is crowned ruler of a country, is a monarch. A monarchy is a government in which a monarch has supreme power. In a large vacant hall or in a thick forest, you can hear the echo of your voice. An echo is a resound. An epoch is an age, period, or fixed time in history.

To bring a schooner or ship to a stop in water, we use an anchor. An anchor is a heavy iron hook. One who compounds chemicals and mixes drugs is a chemist. To become a chemist, one must study chemistry. Phyllis was surprised to learn in her chemistry class that graphite and diamonds have the same chemical formula; yet, because of different molecular structures, one is the softest of minerals and the other the hardest. A skilled worker is a mechanic. A mechanic is a person who is an expert with tools or machinery. Not every one who uses tools is an expert mechanic.

Character is a quality of a person. We judge a person by his character. A person can be of either good or bad character. A person of sterling character is trusted and respected, and a man who schemes, cheats, and lies has a bad character. The letters composing each and every word of these pages are characters. Each letter is a separate character.

## LESSON 95—(Continued)

A chronic disease is a sickness of long duration. A headache, toothache, or stomach-ache is not a chronic disease. Some people with stomach trouble of long standing are said to have a chronic sickness.

The stomach is the organ in the body in which the food we eat is digested. Chronicle is another name for history. A chronicler is one who records history in the order of time it happened. A band of musicians is called an orchestra, and a number of people singing together is called a chorus. A group of singers in a church, temple, or any place of worship is a choir. The choir sings Christmas carols.

## LESSON 96

gn in same syllable, g is silent

In words beginning or ending with gn, g is silent

Words ending in gn, the g remains silent generally when adding the following suffixes: -s, -er, -or, -ee, -ing, -ed, -ment

| gnaw | sign | reign | chignon |
| gnash | assign | feign | consignor |
| gnarl | design | deign | consignee |
| gnats | resign | foreign | consignment |
| gnome | consign | sovereign | foreigner |
| gnu | benign | impugn | signed |
| gnar | aligns | champagne | arraigning |
| gnosis | malign | cologne | campaigning |
| gnathic | ensigns | bologna | alignment |
| gnawed | realign | cognac | sovereignty |
| gnashing | arraign | vignette | cosigner |
| gnarled | campaign | poignant | assignment |

## LESSON 96—(Continued)

> gn not in same syllable, sound both
> (generally when adding any suffix
> except those shown in box on preceding page
> or
> when gn occurs medially in the root word,
> but not in same syllable)

| | | | |
|---|---|---|---|
| signet | signature | designate | malignant |
| signal | resignation | benignant | agnostic |
| signatory | diagnosis | cosignatory | cognizant |
| cognate | signaling | signaled | significant |
| insignia | cognitive | cognition | malignancy |
| prognosis | designation | insignificant | prognosticate |

> gm in same syllable,
> g is silent

phlegm   diaphragm

> gm not in same syllable, sound both

| | | | |
|---|---|---|---|
| phlegmatic | diaphragmatic | stigma | pragmatism |
| astigmatism | pragmatic | dogma | dogmatic |
| quagmire | sigma | enigma | enigmatic |

### EXERCISES

A red light is a sign of caution or to stop. A red flag is a sign of danger. Every contract must be signed by its makers. Checks and documents without signatures are valueless. A signature is a sign of your consent or approval. Signs give us information. The sign over a store

# LESSON 96—(Continued)

tells us to whom it belongs and what we can get in that store. To assign is to appoint or select for a duty. Policemen are assigned to patrol a certain street or place. A military officer is assigned to give orders or to do some other duty.

The teacher gives her pupils daily assignments. The teacher designates the exact lessons she wants the pupils to study. To consign is to deliver or send goods. Goods sent on order is a consignment. The one who sends it is the consignor, and the one who receives the consignment is the consignee. One who designs new styles of dresses and suits is a fashion designer. One who draws patterns for wallpaper and oilcloth is an art designer.

Every fourth year before election we have a presidential campaign. Each national party campaigns for its candidate. A campaign is a continued effort by many to accomplish the same thing. An ensign is the lowest ranking officer in the navy. Ensigns serve on United States battleships. Battleships give orders by signals with flags. To signal is to give a sign. An alarm box is an electric signal system by which we notify or signal the police or the fire department. A signet is a seal or stamp which is used instead of or in addition to a signature. A ring with engraved initial letters is a signet ring.

Some people, though they hear well, for some reason feign to be deaf. Others with good eyesight and perfect vision feign or make believe that they are blind. A foreigner is a stranger belonging to another nation or country. A foreigner speaks a foreign language. Many foreigners flee to our shores from a reign of terror. Those who can't flee must resign themselves to their cruel fate. To reign is to rule or govern. To resign is to yield or submit. The teacher sent in her resignation because of ill health.

# LESSON 97

**wr**
**(w silent)**

| | | | |
|---|---|---|---|
| wrap | wrath | wrinkle | wrought |
| wreck | wreak | writer | wringers |
| wring | wry | written | wretched |
| wrist | wryly | wrecking | wrapped |
| write | wretch | wreckage | wrongly |
| wrote | wrench | wrathful | wrecker |
| wrong | wriggle | wrongful | wreaked |
| wrung | wrest | wringer | unwritten |
| writ | writhe | wreath | unwrinkled |
| wren | wrangle | wreathe | awry |

## EXERCISES

Most people write with their right hand. When you send a parcel by mail, wrap it in heavy wrapping paper. Do not wrinkle the wrapper. You cannot write well on wrinkled paper. Write your own name and address on the upper left hand corner, and lower down to the right, write plainly on the wrapper the name and address of the consignee.

To wring is to twist. Wringing is harmful to some fabrics. Before the invention of the washing machine, laundry was wrung by hand, and this was a tedious, laborious, and time-consuming process. Wringers were standard equipment on the early electric washing machines, and this innovation was a tremendous improvement over wringing by hand. Now the spin cycle, which is quicker and more efficient, has replaced the wringer.

Do what is right; never what is wrong. The teacher said to Willie, "Write wrong." Willie wrote, "Right wrong." The teacher said, "Right is wrong and wrong is right." In a wrestling match, the wrestlers are of about the same weight. Many a wrist was wrenched while

## LESSON 97—(Continued)

wrestling. To wrench is to twist out of joint. A wristwatch is a watch worn on the forearm or wrist.

When riding, don't be a backseat driver and don't be jittery and wriggly. Many wrecks are the result of just that. It might be even worse—a reckless driver, a wreckage on the road, a fresh wreath in the cemetery, and many wretched hearts. A noisy or angry dispute is a wrangle. To wrangle is the same as to quarrel. A wrench is an instrument or tool.

## LESSON 98

**kn
(k silent)**

| | | | |
|---|---|---|---|
| knack | knell | knuckle | unknown |
| knap | knock | knew | knocking |
| knave | knob | known | knotty |
| knead | knit | knotted | knickers |
| knee | knight | knitted | knighthood |
| kneel | knife | knowledge | kneecap |
| knelt | knives | knapsack | kneeled |
| knot | know | acknowledge | kneading |
| knoll | knockout | knickknack | doorknob |

### EXERCISES

Many things we know today were not known a few years ago. We got our knowledge by study and experience. To know that you don't know is a great knowledge. A man of knowledge is one who knows much. To have a knack is to possess the art of doing a thing well. Anybody can make a sale, but not everybody has the knack of making a customer. Some people have the knack of making friends.

# LESSON 98—(Continued)

A knife is a tool or instrument with which we cut. Good knives are made of steel. The butchers use several knives of different lengths and shapes. A jackknife is a pocketknife, sometimes called a boy's knife.

In a knitting mill, they make socks and stockings. Many women knit their own sweaters. To knit is to weave with needles. A knot is weaving or tying together. The knight knocked his knuckles against the doorknob. A knuckle is a finger joint. The baker has to knead the dough well before baking the bread. They used to knead the dough by hand, but now they don't need to knead it by hand. The kneading machine does it much quicker and better.

The joint between the two principal parts of the leg is the knee. To kneel is to go down on the knees; that is, to bend the knees and rest on them.

Once while traveling with his knights in his royal coach, a great king noticed a man on the road who knelt in prayer. The coach came to a halt, and the king and his knights alighted and stepped over to the kneeling man. The man, undisturbed, continued praying. After a while, when the man had finished, he turned and bowed low to greet the king. Wrathfully the king asked, "If you knew that I am the king, why did you not stop to greet me before?" "Your Majesty," said the man, "I knelt before to the King of Kings." "Do you know that disrespect to the king is punishable by death?" asked the king. "Yes, your Majesty, I knew that, too," said the man, "but the fear of the Lord must be greater than the fear of death."

Among the interesting bits of information in Charlotte's scrapbook are the following items: A man kneeling with his arms spread in amazement is the Egyptian hieroglyphic symbol for one million. Barnacles manufacture a glue so tough that it resists all chemicals known to man. The merry-go-round was originated during the Middle Ages as a training device for knights and princes in the sport of ring spearing.

# LESSON 99

**-lk   -lm   -lf   -lve   -ld**
**L silent**

### lk

| | |
|---|---|
| talk | stalk |
| walk | balk |
| calk | balky |
| chalk | walkie-talkie |
| folk | walkie-lookie |
| yolk | chalkboard |

### lm

| | |
|---|---|
| alms | almond |
| balm | salmon |
| calm | embalm |
| malm | balmy |
| palm | qualmish |
| qualm | becalm |

### lf

half
calf
behalf

### lve

halves
calves
salve

### ld

could
would
should
solder

**-lk   -lm   -lf   -lve   -ld**
**When not in same syllable, sound both**

| | | | | |
|---|---|---|---|---|
| seldom | children | Dalmatian | alfalfa | shoulder |
| Thelma | mildew | palmetto | Sylvester | boulder |
| dolman | Waldorf | fulminate | alkali | alkaloid |
| Elmer | Balkan | pulmonary | balderdash | Chaldean |
| elder | pilfer | balmoral | folderol | sulfa |
| Selma | caldron | palmyra | dalmatic | doldrums |

## EXERCISES

Blessed are those who give bread to the poor and alms to the needy. Alms is charitable aid. When you give alms, let not your left hand know what your right hand is doing. Palm trees grow in a warm

## LESSON 99—(Continued)

climate. There are many kinds of palm trees. The palmyra and the palmetto are palm trees. Dates are the fruit of one kind of palm. The inner flat part of the hand is also called the palm. The palm of the hand is from the wrist to the fingers on the side opposite the knuckles. A palmist is one who tells fortunes by the lines of the palm of the hand.

An almond is a kind of nut or the kernel of that fruit. There are sweet and bitter almonds, also soft and hard shelled almonds. Salmon is a food fish. Red salmon is better than pink salmon and therefore more expensive. Balm is a soothing, healing oil. Balm is an aromatic preparation used in embalming the dead. Kind and consoling words are balm to the weary and oppressed. They act as balm to a wound. Salve is an ointment put on a sore to soothe the pain. For every sore there is a certain salve.

To talk is to speak. Idle talk is cheap. It is just chatter or gossip. "Talk less and do more" is a wise motto. Talk reason, talk common sense, but do not try to talk people out of something or into anything. Walk straight and watch your step. A child must learn how to walk first before it can attempt to run. Walking is a healthful exercise. The science teacher told the class that the nuthatch is the only American bird that can walk head first down a tree.

The yolk of an egg is the yellow part of the egg. After a storm there comes calm. After a hard day's work, we enjoy the calm and rest of the night. Beliefs and customs, or popular tales and legends of a people are called "folklore." Songs originated and sung among the common people are "folk-songs." Fifty-fifty is to divide a thing into two equal parts and share it half and half. Two halves make one whole. A calf is the young of a cow. More than one calf is calves. More than one knife is knives.

Two boys had one pie. One of the boys who had a jackknife cut the pie into two unequal parts, took the larger half for himself, and gave the smaller part to his friend. "If I would have divided the pie," said the one with the smaller portion, "I would have given you the bigger piece and would have kept the smaller half for myself." "Well," said the greedy one, "that is just exactly what I did."

# LESSON 100

**-mb**  **-bt**

**b silent**

| lamb | succumb | bombshell | debt |
| limb | limbless | lambskin | doubt |
| bomb | dumbness | benumb | subtle |
| numb | bomber | dumbstruck | debtor |
| thumb | plumber | thumbtack | doubtless |
| dumb | succumbing | plumbing | indebted |
| crumb | bombproof | numbness | subtlety |
| plumb | dumbfound | dumbwaiter | doubtful |
| jamb | succumbed | bombsight | subtlest |
| aplomb | numbing | thumbnail | undoubtedly |

*Non-Phonic:* tomb  womb  climb  comb  catacomb

**When mb is not in same syllable, sound both**

| limbo | combine | limber | crumbling |
| bombard | bombardment | crumbly | remember |
| combat | crumble | combustion | slumber |
| number | bombardier | jamboree | tremble |

**-sten**  **-ften**  **-stle**

**t silent**

| fasten | often | trestle | whistle |
| hasten | soften | bustle | whistling |
| moisten | softeners | bustling | epistle |
| listen | softening | jostle | nestle |

210

## LESSON 100—(Continued)

| | | | |
|---|---|---|---|
| glisten | castle | jostled | nestling |
| mistletoe | gristle | wrestle | apostle |
| christen | gristly | rustle | pestle |
| listener | hustle | rustlers | bristle |
| hastened | hustled | thistle | bristling |

## EXERCISES

A bomb is a hollow shell filled with explosive powder. Our bombardiers dropped heavy bombs on enemy positions. It was a fierce bombardment which lit up the sky and lasted all night. The United States bombers are the fastest and best in the world. To climb is to rise or to go up by the help of the hands and feet. The bombardiers climb into the cockpit of the plane. The painter climbs up on the roof and the fireman climbs up on the ladder.

A comb is a toothed instrument. A comb is a toilet article used for fixing or combing the hair. A crumb is a morsel or very small piece of anything, as a crumb of bread. To crumble is to break into small pieces. Crumbly is brittle or anything we can easily crush into tiny bits. To be in debt is to owe something to another. If you owe, pay your debts on time. A debtor is one who has an obligation to pay. Do not contract new debts before you pay the old ones.

He who doubts does not believe. When in doubt, ask. To doubt is to hesitate to believe. We often have to doubt the truth of a story. We distrust a person of doubtful character. Doubtless is a fact free from doubt. If the fingers are numb, one cannot write. In severe cold, the toes get numb. Any part of the body deprived of feeling is numb. The thick short finger of either hand is the thumb. A child born deaf will also be dumb. One who cannot talk is dumb. A dull or stupid person is called dumb. "Be kind to dumb animals." When we say dumb animals, we do not mean stupid animals. Animals are intelligent and often display good judgement. By dumb we simply mean that animals cannot talk as we can.

## LESSON 100—(Continued)

The plumber installs the heating system in our homes. The plumber puts in and fits pipes for gas, water and sewers in the buildings. George Washington's tomb is in Arlington National Cemetery. The tombs of the unknown servicemen are also in that same cemetery. A tomb is a grave.

Once a man had a large orchard of luscious fruit. To make sure that no one, not even the watchman, would steal any, he employed two men. One was blind, so he could not see the fruit, and the other was without a limb, so he could not climb the trees. Said the limbless man to the blind one, "If I climb on your shoulders, you'll carry me where I'll direct you. I'll be your eyes and hands, and you'll be my feet. We can thus get the fruit and neither one of us will be blamed for it." "Yes," said the blind man, "neither one will be blamed, but both of us will be hanged."

## LESSON 101

h silent

| ghost | rheumatic | heirloom | honorable |
| ghastly | herb | honor | herbage |
| Rhine | hour | honest | heiress |
| rhyme | hourly | honesty | rhapsody |
| rhythm | heir | honestly | rhetoric |
| rhubarb | exhort | exhibition | exhaustion |
| rheostat | exhibit | catarrh | rheumatism |
| gherkin | dahlia | rhinoceros | posthumous |
| dinghy | spaghetti | jodhpurs | exhilarate |
| myrrh | pyorrhea | ghoul | ghetto |

## LESSON 101—(Continued)

| ps | pn | pt |
|---|---|---|
| | p silent | |

| | | | |
|---|---|---|---|
| psychic | psychedelic | pneumonia | ptomaine |
| psalm | psychiatry | pneumatic | pteridophyte |
| pseudonym | psychology | pneumectomy | ptosis |
| psittacosis | psoriasis | pneumococcus | Ptolemy |
| psalmody | psychosomatic | pneumograph | pteridology |
| psalmist | psychoanalyze | pneumothorax | pterodactyl |
| psalter | psychotherapy | pneumatology | pteropod |
| psychosis | psychodynamic | pneumoconiosis | pterosaur |

## EXERCISES

"Honesty is the best policy." A person who is true, upright, just, and fair in dealing with others in word and action is an honest man. An honest person is of good and sincere character. "Honor thy father and thy mother." Honor is respect and reverence blended together. One who is worthy to be trusted is honorable.

The days of the year are divided into twenty-four parts. Each part is called an "hour." There are sixty minutes in every hour. Every hour is a milestone in a person's life. Take good care of your hours, and the years will take care of themselves.

One of the longest words in the dictionary is pneumonoultramicroscopicsilicovolcanoconiosis. It means a disease of the lungs caused by the inhalation of very fine silicate or quartz dust. Rhett learned in his biology class that the great rhinoceros beetle can lift 850 times its own weight, which is comparable to an elephant's lifting a small ship.

A battlefield, with hundreds of bodies of men strewn around, is a ghastly sight to behold. But as ghastly as war is, we liberty-loving people would rather fight and die on our feet than live on our knees. To give up the ghost is to die. The ghost is the spirit or soul of man. Ghost stories are weird tales about the soul of a dead person, believed by some people to wander around or haunt the living.

## LESSON 101—(Continued)

An heir is one who inherits or succeeds to the estate after a person's death. Children are the legal heirs to their parents' possessions. An heiress is a female heir. Any personal possession or article that passes over from generation to generation in the same family is an heirloom. It is not so much the value of the article as the memories and history attached to the heirloom that we prize so highly. Green vegetables and plants, not woody like trees and shrubs, are herbs. Herbage is vegetation or pasturage like grass and clover. Rhubarb is an herb or plant used for food and also used as a drug or medicine.

A young man, who became the sole heir to his father's great fortune, ordered all his employees to start work one hour earlier than they used to while his father managed the business. One old employee refused to do so. When asked by his new boss the reason why, the old timer explained, "You see, when you come earlier, you feel rich an hour sooner; but if I would come earlier every day, I would have to feel a whole hour sooner that, in spite of my many years of honest toil, I am still poor."

## LESSON 102

mn
n silent

| hymn | column | solemn | autumn |
| condemn | condemned | solemnly | damn |

mn
When not in the same syllable, sound both

| hymnal | condemnation | damnation |
| columnist | condemnatory | solemnity |
| autumnal | columnar | solemnize |

# LESSON 102—(Continued)

## EXERCISES

Autumn is the third season of the year. The period of three months between summer and winter is autumn. The better known name of autumn is "fall," because it is the season when the leaves are falling off the trees. An elderly person, past middle age and not yet very old, is said to be in the autumn of life. Fruits that ripen and are gathered late in September are autumnal fruits.

To damn something is to condemn it. Damnation is the same as condemnation. Damn and damnation are used frequently in the Bible. To condemn is to convict, to find a person guilty of a crime, and to sentence him to punishment. To condemn is to express judgement against someone. Do not condemn a person before you know all the particulars about him. A condemned murderer is a person found guilty of a horrible crime and he deserves condemnation.

A religious holiday is a solemn occasion. A sacred ceremony is a solemn rite. When a public officer, such as a president or governor, takes the oath of office, he says, "I do solemnly swear . . . ." An impressive, awe-inspiring ceremony is carried out with solemnity. The dedication of a new church, temple, house of worship, hospital, or charitable home is a solemn occasion, and those present witness the ceremony in solemnity. A wedding is usually solemnized in a church or temple. In a house of worship, we sing hymns. We stand in deep respect when the national hymn or anthem, "The Star Spangled Banner," is played or sung. A collection or book of hymns is called a hymnal.

A column is a pillar. The roof of a porch rests on columns. The columns we see in front of old colonial buildings are of iron, stone, or marble. Newspaper pages are divided into columns; that is, the lines do not run across the entire page. A formation of troops is a column. In a public celebration, the marchers form in columns. One who writes a daily article in a newspaper is called a columnist.

# LESSON 103

### que at the end of a word
### (q as k and ue silent. - - que as k)

| | | | |
|---|---|---|---|
| antique | burlesque | physique | oblique |
| grotesque | boutique | arabesque | pique |
| plaque | unique | catafalque | piquing |
| torque | mosque | mystique | picturesque |
| statuesque | critique | clique | brusque |
| humoresque | critiquing | opaque | discotheque |

### qu as k

| | | | |
|---|---|---|---|
| croquette | etiquette | lacquer | conquer |
| coquette | briquette | coquina | tourniquet |
| marquee | mosquito | liquor | unconquerable |
| piquant | quiche | mannequin | masquerade |

### que and quet as "kay"

| | | | |
|---|---|---|---|
| communique | applique | parquet | sobriquet |
| risque | pique | croquet | bouquet |

### gue at the end of a word
### (g hard, ue silent. - - gue as hard g)

| | | | |
|---|---|---|---|
| fatigue | monologue | harangue | colleague |
| intrigue | dialogue | tongue | rogue |
| decalogue | catalogue | league | vogue |
| prologue | demagogue | morgue | vague |
| epilogue | pedagogue | brogue | plague |
| analogue | synagogue | fugue | meringue |

*Exception:* argue

# LESSON 103—(Continued)

### gu as gw

| | | | |
|---|---|---|---|
| linguist | sanguine | jaguar | consanguinity |
| language | anguish | languish | linguistics |
| penguin | inguinal | guava | distinguish |
| iguana | languid | extinguish | iguanadon |

### gu as hard g

| | | | |
|---|---|---|---|
| guest | roguish | languor | guerrilla |
| guessed | guide | guilt | guillotine |
| guard | guidance | guise | guinea |
| guy | guild | guaranteed | disguise |
| beguile | guile | guarantor | guilty |
| guitar | guardian | guaranty | beleaguer |

### u as w

| | | | |
|---|---|---|---|
| persuade | suede | suite | persuasion |
| assuage | pueblo | suave | dissuade |

### o as w
### oi as wah    oua as wa

| | | | |
|---|---|---|---|
| coiffure | boudoir | bivouac | bourgeois |
| coiffeur | memoir | coiffeuse | bourgeoisie |

217

# LESSON 103—(Continued)
## EXERCISES

An article of very great age, anything of long, long ago, is an antique. In an antique store, we may find a book that dates back to the time when printing was first invented. We may find a piece of furniture several centuries old. Real antiques are of great value because of their age or because they are unique.

When a thing is very rare, or the only one in existence, or unusual, we say it is unique. The articles in an antique store are catalogued. A catalogue is an illustrated price list in which, in addition to the cost, a description of each article is listed. Book stores, too, have catalogues.

A mosque is a Mohammedan temple or place of worship, just like a church. A synagogue is a Jewish temple. Some people know no fatigue. They never get tired or weary. They build and toil for the good of others. Fatigue is bodily or mental exhaustion. Every child should know the Decalogue by memory. Decalogue is another name for the Ten Commandments. The Decalogue is the foundation upon which all good and just laws are built.

A demagogue is a popular orator or speaker who has no principle or feeling for others. A demagogue is a person who tries to mislead people by telling them things the wrong way. The purpose of the demagogue is to intrigue. To intrigue is to secretly plot or scheme against the innocent.

Christopher found the following interesting items in a book he was reading: During the Middle Ages, a king often greeted guests while he was still in bed. Chinese is one of the few languages that cannot be adapted for use in crossword puzzles. The largest antique ever sold is the London Bridge, which was moved from London, England, to Lake Havasu City, Arizona, in 1968. Penguins can leap at least six feet out of the water.

One whose occupation is the instruction of children is a pedagogue. A pedagogue is a teacher. A monologue is a recitation done by one person alone, but if two persons take part in it, it is a dialogue. Some stage plays or motion picture plays begin with a prologue. A prologue is an introduction to the play, and an epilogue is an addition at the end of the play or show.

# THE TONGUE

Once a wise man was asked what he thought was the best meat, and he answered, "The tongue." "And what is the worst meat?" Again he answered, "The tongue." When he was asked to explain how a thing can be the best and the worst at the same time, he told the following story:

The daughter of a mighty ruler was very ill. The best physicians in the country attended the princess, but none could find the cause of her sickness and therefore could give her no relief. After many months, a specialist prescribed "milk of a lioness." "Milk of a lioness" was not a medicine that money could buy, nor was it a preparation kept on the shelves of a drugstore. It required patience, skill, and the risk of one's life to catch a lioness and milk her. The king, therefore, offered a great reward to anyone who would undertake to do it. Soon a young man, eager to save the beautiful princess, declared his willingness to brave the danger. He equipped himself and, with a crew of men, left for the jungle.

The journey was crowned with success, his mission carried through to fulfillment, and the young man was on his way back with a cruse of the coveted milk. Tired from the heat of the day and the wearisome travel, he fell asleep. He slept and dreamt a peculiar dream.

All the parts of his body argued with each other. His feet claimed to have earned the reward, because if it weren't for them, the rest of his body could not have gotten to the lioness. His hands argued that the reward belonged to them, because it was the hands that captured and milked the lioness. But his eyes claimed that without their guidance, he would never have reached the jungle, nor found the lioness, and so he would not have been able to get the milk. Then his heart spoke up and said, "All of you take a rest sometimes, while I am forever on the alert and never rest, working at all times, supplying all of you with strength and courage, without which you could not exist at all." Lastly, the tongue spoke up, "The reward belongs to me." All the parts laughed at the tongue saying, "What have you done to earn it?" The tongue answered, "Wait and you will see that everything depends upon me."

# THE TONGUE—(Continued)

The man woke up somewhat troubled by this strange dream and hurried homeward to take the cure to the princess as quickly as possible. As soon as he reached the palace, he was led before the king and reported, "Your Majesty, I have brought the milk of the dog." Before he had time to correct the slip of his tongue, the king called out in great rage, "What, the milk of a dog!" He ordered his guards to chain the culprit and put him to death the very next day. Stunned and terrified by this sudden change of fate, the erstwhile hero felt crushed as if struck by a thunderbolt from a clear sky.

Alone in his cell and agonizing over the swift turn of events, slumber came to the rescue of the doomed man. He slept and dreamt again. He dreamed that every part of his body quarreled with his tongue. "It is you who brought suffering and death upon all of us," they told the wicked tongue. "It is because of your having changed the word 'lioness' to 'dog' that all of us will be killed." "Sure," answered the tongue, "sure it is because of me, but you all laughed at me when I said that life and death, reward and punishment depend upon me."

At this the doomed man awoke, trembling in every fiber of his body. He now recalled his first dream and thoroughly understood its meaning. He immediately asked permission to say a few words to the king before his death. This permission was granted to him, and he told the king of the two dreams he had had. The king realized now that the word "dog" was a mere slip of the tongue and readily pardoned the gallant, courageous young hero. The princess got well and all were happy again.

"Lord, I pray Thee, guard my tongue from uttering evil and my lips from speaking guile."

---

*"If thou lackest knowledge,*
*What hast thou?*
*If thou hast knowledge,*
*What lackest thou?"*

# HOMONYMS

*Words Pronounced Alike, or Almost Alike, But Different in Spelling and Meaning.*

*Ate:* Did eat, partook of food. We *ate* our lunch.
*Eight:* Twice four, the number after seven, 8. *Eight.*

*Ail:* To suffer, to be in pain, to have an ache. Judging from the expression on his face, something seems to *ail* the man.
*Ale:* A malt liquor, brewed beverage. He likes ginger *ale.*

*An:* Indefinite article, like *an* armful, *an* apple.
*Ann:* A name of a woman or girl.

*Air:* The atmosphere. We breathe fresh *air.*
*Heir:* One who inherits. He is the sole *heir* to the fortune his father left.
*Ere:* Before. Think *ere* you speak. We will be back *ere* long.

*All:* The whole. At *all* times, *all* day, *all* of us.
*Awl:* A tool to make holes; a tool shoemakers use. A shoemaker uses an *awl* to pierce holes in leather.

*Altar:* A place of offerings in a church, temple, or synagogue. The bride and groom met at the *altar.*
*Alter:* To change. I shall *alter* my last year's dress.

*Bail:* Surety, security given for a prisoner's release; to clear from a boat by dipping and throwing; to parachute from an airplane. A bonding company offered *bail* for $1,000. He *bailed* out of the plane. They *bailed* the water out of the boat.
*Bale:* A large bundle. A *bale* of hay; a *bale* of scrap paper; a *bale* of cotton.

*Bare:* Naked. *Bare* headed; *bare* foot, *bare* hands.
*Bear:* An animal; to carry, to suffer, to *bear* the burden. I can *bear* no more pain.

*Be:* To exist. "To *be* or not to *be.*" *Be* here on time.
*Bee:* The insect that makes honey. She is as busy as a *bee.*

# HOMONYMS—(Continued)

*Beet:* A vegetable, a red *beet,* sugar *beet.*
*Beat:* To strike, to outdo. Don't *beat* a dumb animal. His heart still *beats*. I can *beat* him running.

*Berry:* A small fruit. Straw*berry,* black*berry,* etc.
*Bury:* To inter, to deposit, to put in a grave. We *bury* the dead.

*Bred:* Educated, brought up. He is a well-*bred* man.
*Bread:* An article of food. We work for our *bread*.

*By:* Near, at, about, per. We work *by* the week. We will get there *by* noon.
*Buy:* Purchase. I *buy* my bread from the baker. We *buy* and sell used cars.
*Bye:* Good*bye!*

*Born:* Came into existence. I was *born* in this country. He was *born* in May.
*Borne:* Was carried. The man was *borne* away by policemen.

*Blue:* A color. Red, white, and *blue*. The sky is *blue*.
*Blew:* Made a fast current of air. A strong wind *blew*. He *blew* his horn.

*Berth:* A sleeping place. I slept in an upper *berth*.
*Birth:* Act of coming into life. She gave *birth* to a baby. The *birth* of a new idea.

*Cain:* A man's name. *Cain* slew his brother Abel.
*Cane:* A walking stick; various bamboolike grasses. The old man walks with a *cane*. Sugar *cane* is a stout, tall perennial grass extensively cultivated in warm regions for its sugar.

*Choose:* To select, to prefer. You will have to *choose* which one to take.
*Chews:* Does *chew,* grinds the food with the teeth. He *chews* his food well.

# HOMONYMS—(Continued)

*Capital:* Chief city of a state or country; invested wealth. Washington is the *capital* of the United States. He invested a large *capital* in the business.

*Capitol:* Legislative building. The *capitol* building of each state is located in its *capital* city. Congress meets in the *capitol* in Washington, D.C.

*Cell:* Small room, as in a prison. The convict was locked in a *cell*.

*Sell:* To part with for a price. I'll *sell* you my house cheap. We *sell* fresh eggs and butter.

*Cellar:* An underground room. Wine is kept in a *cellar*.

*Seller:* One who sells, a dealer in merchandise. The *seller* made a profit on the sale of his automobile.

*Cent:* A copper coin. One hundredth of a dollar. Not worth a *cent*. A cent is the smallest unit of United States money.

*Scent:* Odor, perfume, smell. The dog can *scent* his way home.

*Sent:* Did send. I was *sent* here. I *sent* you money last week.

*Dear:* Beloved; costly. My *dear* friend. It is too *dear* to waste.

*Deer:* A swift running animal with branching horns. The hunter shot a *deer*.

*Dew:* Falling vapor, moisture falling after sunset. It looks like *dew* drops on the flowers.

*Due:* Time for arrival or payment. The plane is *due* here at 10:30 a.m. Your note in the bank is *due* on the first.

*Do:* Make, perform. I *do* a good deed every day.

*Die:* To expire; to perish; to cease to live. Everything that lives must *die*.

*Dye:* To color, to stain, coloring matter. We *dye* and clean suits and dresses.

# HOMONYMS—(Continued)

*Earn:* To gain, as wages for labor; to merit. I *earn* my bread by honest labor.

*Urn:* A container, a vessel. The ashes of the cremated body were placed in an *urn*.

*End:* Terminal, finish, extreme limit, outcome. All things have a beginning and an *end*. We live in the East *End*. All's well that *ends* well.

*And:* Also, too. I hope you are well *and* happy. He *and* she are my friends.

*Except:* To leave out, to omit, unless. We go to work every day *except* Sunday. I know all my lessons *except* one.

*Accept:* To receive, to take. Please *accept* my thanks. Never *accept* a bribe.

*Excess:* Overflow, more than enough, too much. They sent us food in *excess* of our needs. Never eat or drink to *excess*.

*Access:* An approach, a way to attain, to reach. I had no *access* to him personally. Only the president had *access* to the safe.

*Exceed:* To go beyond. Do not *exceed* the speed limit.

*Accede:* To comply with. He tries to *accede* to her wishes.

*Fair:* Clear, beautiful, not cloudy; just; a market held at certain times. Tomorrow will be *fair* and warmer. Be *fair* with everyone. I want a *fair* deal. We all went to the State *Fair*.

*Fare:* Food ready for the table; cost of passage on a plane, bus, railroad, etc. In a lunchroom, you will find a bill-of-*fare* on each table. Pay your *fare* when you enter the bus.

*Find:* Discover; to meet with. It is easy to lose but hard to *find* a good job.

*Fined:* Money penalty or money paid for an offense. The man was *fined* five dollars for driving his car past a red light.

*Flea:* An insect. This *flea* powder will rid the dog of *fleas*.

*Flee:* To run away, to escape. We had to *flee* for safety. The fire fighters made the women and children *flee* to the mountains.

## HOMONYMS—(Continued)

*For:* In behalf of, because of, on account, to the amount of. I came *for* you and *for* the children. Please do it *for* my sake. We pay cash *for* everything.

*Fore:* Before, front, as *fore*man, *fore*noon, *fore*arm, *fore*head, *fore*tell, *fore*sight.

*Four:* Twice two, the number 4. At *four* p.m. our foreman sent *four* men *for* refreshments, *for* it was very hot all *fore*noon.

*Flash:* A sudden burst of light, to light up suddenly. Every policeman has to carry a *flash*light while on duty. We were blinded by a *flash* of lightning.

*Flesh:* Meat. They are the children of my *flesh* and blood.

*Faith:* Belief; trust in the honesty of another; religion. I have *faith* in my country. She has *faith* in him.

*Fate:* Destiny, foreordained lot, predestined fortune. We are all in the hands of *fate*. Whatever *fate* decrees, we cannot change.

*Guessed:* Hit upon another's thought, surmised. How did you know? I just *guessed*. You *guessed* right.

*Guest:* A visitor, one entertained at another's house. We had the mayor as our *guest*. The speaker is a *guest* in the city.

*Grease:* Rendered fat, oily matter. We fry chicken in *grease* and cook it in water. We *grease* the wheels to make them move easier.

*Greece:* A country in Europe. That man was born in *Greece*. He can speak the Greek language.

*Grate:* A fireplace; to rub. On a cool evening, we make a fire in the *grate*. I hate to *grate* horseradish. It causes my eyes to tear.

*Great:* Large, famous. George Washington was a *great* general. We honor our *great* men.

*Groan:* A low cry of distress. I heard him *groan* and ran to his aid.

*Grown:* Increased in size, reached the limit in height. He is not a child, but a full *grown* person.

# HOMONYMS—(Continued)

*Had:* Past tense of have, possessed. I *had* five dollars, but now I have only fifty cents.

*Head:* The topmost part of the body; chief, leader. He had no hat on his *head*. He sits at the *head* of the table. He is the *head* of his department.

*Hair:* The natural covering of the head or the skin of an animal. The barber cut my *hair* too short.

*Hare:* An animal, a rodent. A rabbit is a small, long-eared mammal of the *hare* family. A *hare* is born furred, while a rabbit is not. Also, the burrowing habits of the *hare* and the rabbit are different.

*Hard:* Solid, firm; not easy, difficult. I work *hard*. *Hard* as a nut. *Hard* to get a job.

*Heart:* The blood pump, a vital inner organ. He has a kind *heart*. He had a *heart* attack and died.

*Hear:* To perceive with the ear, to listen; to obey. Most people *hear* with both ears. He who cannot *hear* is deaf.

*Here:* In this place, at this point. I came *here* to study. We moved *here* to hear the speech better.

*Heal:* Cure, restore to health, get well again. The wound will *heal*. I hope his sore foot will *heal* soon.

*Heel:* The hinderpart of the foot, opposite the toes; the lift on a shoe. The *heel* of my right foot is sore. The rubber *heel* of one shoe fell off.

*He'll:* A contraction for "he will." *He'll* do the job well. *He'll* wear a shoe as soon as his *heel heals*.

*Heard:* Did hear, was informed. I *heard* good news today. Yes, I *heard* him say that.

*Herd:* Crowd together, many cattle feeding or being together. He has a *herd* of cows on his farm. They drove a *herd* of oxen to the market.

# HOMONYMS—(Continued)

*Higher:* More elevated, loftier, more exalted. My friend was promoted to a *higher* position. We now can fly *higher* than the highest mountain.

*Hire:* To rent, to lease, to engage for service. We can *hire* all the help we need. Horses and mules for *hire*. I'll *hire* a maid who can cook, too.

*Hole:* A cavity, hollow place, pit. We dug a deep *hole* and struck water. I have a *hole* in my pocket.

*Whole:* All, complete, sound, unbroken. We occupy the *whole* house. I'll buy a *whole* basket of tomatoes.

*Holy:* Sinless, sacred, pious, saintly. The *Holy* Bible. A person morally good and pure is a *holy* person.

*Wholly:* Altogether, entirely. This building is for rent *wholly* or in part.

*Loose:* Not fast, not tight. Don't let the dog *loose*. This screw is *loose*.

*Lose:* Cease to have; defeated. We must not *lose* our temper. We did not *lose* the war.

## CONSONANT SOUNDS

| Name of Consonant | Name of Consonant Spelled Phonetically | How To Say Sound Of Consonant | | | Sound of Consonant When Not Part of Consonant's Name |
|---|---|---|---|---|---|
| | | Say Name of Consonant | Don't Say Vowel Part of Consonant's Name | | |
| B | bee | bee | - minus ee | - b~~ee~~ | |
| C | see | see | - minus ee | - s~~ee~~ (soft sound) | |
| | | (Hard sound of C is same as K) | | | |
| D | dee | dee | - minus ee | - d~~ee~~ | |
| F | ef | ef | - minus e | - ~~e~~f | |
| G | jee | jee | - minus ee | - j~~ee~~ (soft sound) | |
| | | (Hard sound is as in word "gag.") | | | |
| H | aich | | | | Single utterance of voiceless exhalation sound of person out of breath. |
| J | jay | jay | - minus ay | - j~~ay~~ | |
| K | kay | kay | - minus ay | - k~~ay~~ | |
| | | (Also hard sound of C) | | | |
| L | el | el | - minus e | - ~~e~~l | |
| M | em | em | - minus e | - ~~e~~m | |
| N | en | en | - minus e | - ~~e~~n | |
| P | pee | pee | - minus ee | - p~~ee~~ | |
| Q | kue | kue | - minus ue | - k~~ue~~ | |
| R | ahr | ahr | - minus ah | - ~~ah~~r | |
| S | ess | ess | - minus e | - ~~e~~ss | Can also sound like Z. |
| T | tee | tee | - minus ee | - t~~ee~~ | |
| V | vee | vee | - minus ee | - v~~ee~~ | |
| W | double U | | | | Like long oo blended into vowel sound which always follows it. |
| X | eks | eks | - minus e | - ~~e~~ks | |
| | | (Prefix ex- followed by a vowel frequently sounds like "eggs," as EXIST.) | | | |
| | | (X at beginning of word has same sound as Z; example: xylophone.) | | | |
| Y | wie | | | | Like ee or short i, blended into vowel sound which always follows it. (Rule: Y is a consonant when it begins a word or begins a syllable and is followed by a vowel.) |
| | | | | | (NOTE: Y as a vowel has the same sounds as I, both long and short.) |
| Z | zee | zee | - minus ee | - z~~ee~~ | |

# INDEX

## Abbreviations: L., Lesson; p., page

### A

a—L. 1, p. 11
a (as in "all" or short "o" sound in wa, war, qua, quar, wha, whar)—L. 60, p. 123
a (five sounds of a)—L. 58, p. 119
a long: (See also under actual letter combinations.) L. 2, p. 12; L. 4, p. 14; L. 9, p. 21
  ange as ainge—L. 77, p. 161
  before r; air, -are—L. 57, p. 117
  ea as long a—L. 64, p. 134
  ei as long a—L. 80, p. 167
  eigh; ei as long a, gh silent—L. 80, p. 167
  ey as long a—L. 80, p. 167
  two consonants at beginning of word—L. 37, p. 70
  two consonants at end of word—L. 25, p. 50
a- (prefix), two-syllable words—L. 52, p. 105
a short:
  L. 13, p. 29
  before r; ar sounded as r—L. 58, p. 119
  short a sound in arr, ara, are, ari, aro, aru, ary, before end of root word—L. 59, p. 121
  two consonants at beginning of word—L. 38, p. 71
  two consonants at beginning and two at end of word—L. 38, p. 72
  two consonants at end of word—L. 25, p. 50
abbreviations:
  a.m., A.M.—L. 11, p. 25
  etc.—L. 73, p. 152
  Mr.—L. 18, p. 38
  Mrs.—L. 18, p. 38
  Ms.—L. 18, p. 38
  p.m., P.M.—L. 11, p. 25
adjective endings (-ous, -an)—L. 74, p. 155
--ae as long a—L. 4, p. 14
a_e as long a—L. 4, p. 14
ai as long a—L. 2, p. 12
ai - both vowels sounded—L. 92, p. 194
ai - ia—L. 92, p. 190
air:
  long a before r—L. 57, p. 117
  sound spelled ear as in bear—L. 64, p. 135
al—L. 56, p. 115
"all" sound—L. 56, p. 115
alphabet—L. 36, p. 69
-an ending indicates person, adjective, or geographical location—L. 74, p. 155
anecdotes: (See also jokes, riddles, and stories.)
  Andrew, the mischievous boy, in Sunday School—L. 91, p. 189
  Boy always late to school—L. 83, p. 173
  Boy who forgot things—L. 66, p. 139
  City dude heckling manager of country store—L. 78, p. 165
  Fatty and Texas tease each other—L. 49, p. 99
  Girl who came to work late—L. 83, p. 173
  Man who inherited his father's business—L. 101, p. 214
  Teacher asks Jennie to name wild animals—L. 69, p. 145
  Two boys and the pie—L. 99, p. 209
  Watchmen and the orchard—L. 100, p. 212
  "Write wrong," teacher asks Willie—L. 97, p. 205
ange as ainge—L. 77, p. 161
ao:
  ao - oa—L. 92, p. 190
  both vowels sounded—L. 92, p. 190
ar:
  slurred like er—L. 62, p. 131
  sound spelled ear as in heart—L. 64, p. 135
  sounded as r—L. 58, p. 119
ara—L. 59, p. 121
-are:
  long a before r—L. 57, p. 117
  sound of "a" in "at" and schwa sound—L. 59, p. 121
ari—L. 59, p. 121
aro—L. 59, p. 121
arr—L. 59, p. 121
aru—L. 59, p. 121
ary—L. 59, p. 121
au:
  L. 86, p. 178
  au - ua—L. 92, pp. 191-192
aw:
  L. 86, p. 178
  ough as aw sound, as in thought—L. 87, p. 180
  sound spelled ou as in brought—L. 89, p. 184
--ay as long a:
  L. 9, p. 21
  --ay as ai—L. 9, p. 21
  Introduction to L. 44, p. 85
  ay - ya—L. 92, p. 191

### B

b—L. 8, p. 20
b silent:
  -bt in same syllable—L. 100, p. 210
  -mb in same syllable—L. 100, p. 210
  -bt not in same syllable, sound both—L. 100, p. 210

### C

c hard and soft—L. 78, p. 164
c hard (k sound):
  L. 19, p. 39

## INDEX—(Continued)

c hard (k sound): (continued)
   more-than-one-syllable words—L. 52, p. 106
c (replacement of) in ck after short vowel—
   L. 25, p. 50
c soft (as s):
   L. 72, p. 149; L. 73, p. 151; L. 78, p. 164
   after soft c, e is sounded in -es—L. 72, p. 150
c (use ei after c)—L. 81, p. 168
-cand (verbs ending in -fy and -ly, long y changed to short i when suffix is added)—L. 83, p. 172
-cate (verbs ending in -fy and -ly, long y changed to short i when suffix is added)—L. 83, p. 172
-cation (verbs ending in -fy and -ly, long y changed to short i when suffix is added)—L. 83, p. 172
ce as sh—L. 74, p. 155
ce (soft c)—L. 72, p. 149
ch:
   L. 31, p. 61
   after ch, suffix -es forms a syllable—L. 49, p. 98
   as k—L. 95, p. 200
   as sh—L. 95, p. 200
   before -ed (suffix), e silent, d with sound of t—L. 47, p. 94
   silent—L. 95, p. 200
   ti sounded as ch after s—L. 75, p. 157
chart of consonant sounds—p. 228
chu sound (spelled tu; not in first syllable of root word; long u construction)—L. 79, p. 166
ci:
   as sh—L. 74, p. 154
   as shee—L. 74, p. 154
   c soft—L. 73, p. 151
-cial as shul, shal—L. 74, p. 154
-cian as shun, shan—L. 74, p. 154
-ciate as "she ate"—L. 74, p. 155
-ciency as shunsee, shensee—L. 74, p. 154
-cient as shunt, shent—L. 74, p. 154
-cious as shus—L. 74, p. 154
ck:
   as k—L. 19, p. 39
   before suffix -ed, e silent, d with sound of t—L. 47, p. 94
   one-syllable words—L. 52, p. 106
   replacement of c in ck after short vowel—L. 25, p. 50
   replacement of k in ck after short vowel—L. 25, p. 50
compound consonants—Part III—L. 93, p. 197, through L. 103, p. 217
compound, diphthong, or long vowel combinations, both vowels sounded—L. 92, p. 194
compound vowels—Part III—L. 84, p. 174, through L. 92, p. 194
compound vowels and diphthongs backwards, both vowels sounded—L. 92, pp. 191-192

Consonant Sounds (chart)—p. 228
consonant y—L. 24, p. 48
consonants (three):
   at beginning of word, scr-, spl-, spr-, str-, squ—L. 55, p. 113
   at end of word—L. 55, p. 114
consonants (two):
   at end of word:
     long a—L. 25, p. 50
     long e—L. 26, p. 52
     long o—L. 28, p. 55
     short a—L. 25, p. 50
     short e—L. 26, p. 52
     short i—L. 27, p. 54
     short o—L. 28, p. 55
     short u—L. 29, p. 57
     words with long i without a second vowel, -ild, -ind—L. 69, p. 144
     words with long o without a second vowel, -old, -olt, -ost, -oll—L. 70, p. 146
   separately-sounded at beginning of word:
     long a—L. 37, p. 70
     long e—L. 39, p. 73
     long i—L. 41, p. 76
     long o—L. 42, p. 78
     long u—L. 43, p. 80
     long y—L. 43, p. 80
     short a—L. 38, p. 71
     short e—L. 40, p. 75
     short i—L. 41, p. 77
     short o—L. 42, p. 79
     short u—L. 43, p. 81
   separately-sounded at beginning and two at end of word:
     short a—L. 38, p. 72
     short e—L. 40, p. 75
     short i—L. 41, p. 77
     short o—L. 42, p. 79
     short u—L. 43, p. 81
     short y—L. 43, p. 81
Contents, Table of—unnumbered pages 7-9
contractions:
   I'll—L. 4, p. 14
   he'll—L. 5, p. 15
   there's—L. 14, p. 31
   they're—L. 14, p. 31
   won't—L. 22, p. 45
   you'll—L. 24, p. 48
   you're—L. 24, p. 48
   you've—L. 24, p. 48
cy (c soft)—L. 73, p. 151

### D

d:
   L. 6, p. 16
   after short vowel, insert d before soft g, if word ends in ge followed by consonant which is part of root word—L. 77, p. 161

## INDEX—(Continued)

d as t (suffix -ed, after x, f, s, sh, ch, p, k, ck)—
  L. 47, p. 94
d sound:
  -ed, suffix—L. 47, pp. 93-94
  -ld in same syllable, 1 silent—L. 99, p. 208
de- (prefix)—L. 53, p. 109
dge—L. 77, p. 161
digraph, long vowel: (See also under actual letter combinations.)
  backwards (both vowels sounded)—L. 92, pp. 190-191
  when not at end of root word, both vowels sounded—L. 92, p. 193
diphthongs: (See also under actual letter combinations.)
  backwards (both vowels sounded)—L. 92, pp. 191-192
  both vowels sounded—L. 92, p. 194
double suffixes—L. 71, p. 148
Drill—Long and short vowels (following L. 60)—p. 127

### E

e:
  L. 1, p. 11
  c soft when followed by e—L. 72, p. 149
  dropped when adding suffix -ing—L. 46, p. 91; L. 71, p. 148
  g soft when followed by e—L. 77, p. 161
  long: (See also under actual letter combinations.)
    L. 1, p. 11; L. 3, p. 13; L. 4, p. 14; L. 5, p. 15; L. 64, p. 134
    and long a, side by side, both sounded (as in create)—L. 64, p. 135
    and schwa a, side by side, both sounded (as in area)—L. 64, p. 135
    and short a, side by side, both sounded (as in react)—L. 64, p. 135
    ei or ie—L. 81, pp. 168-169
    --ie—two-syllable words—L. 45, p. 89
    two consonants at beginning of word—L. 39, p. 73
    two consonants at end of word—L. 26, p. 52
    --y (long e or short i sound) in suffix -ly—Introduction to L. 44, p. 85
  Retain e after soft g when next letter is not i or y—L. 77, p. 162
  short:
    L. 14, p. 31
    spelled ea—L. 64, p. 134
    suffix -ed after d and t—L. 48, p. 96
    suffix -es after a hissing sound—L. 49, p. 98
    suffix -es after s, sh, x, z, ch—L. 49, p. 98
    two consonants at beginning of word—L. 40, p. 75
    two consonants at beginning and two at end of word—L. 40, p. 75

e short: (continued)
  two consonants at end of word—L. 26, p. 52
e silent:
  suffix -ed—L. 47, pp. 93-94
  suffix -es, when not after hissing sounds: s, sh, x, z, ch—L. 49, p. 98
--e as long e—L. 4, p. 14
ea:
  as long a—L. 64, p. 134
  as long e—L. 3, p. 13; L. 64, p. 134
  as short e—L. 64, p. 134
  both vowels sounded—L. 64, p. 135; L. 92, p. 194
  seven sounds—L. 64, pp. 134-135
ear:
  as air—L. 64, p. 135
  as ar—L. 64, p. 135
  followed by a consonant, sounded as er—L. 62, p. 130; L. 64, p. 135
-ed suffix:
  e of -ed sounded after d and t—L. 48, p. 96
  e silent, d sound—L. 47, p. 93
  e silent, d with sound of t, after x, f, s, sh, ch, p, k, ck—L. 47, p. 94
ee as long e—L. 3, p. 13
e_e as long e—L. 5, p. 15
ei:
  as ee (long e) after c and sometimes after s—L. 81, pp. 168-169
  as long a—L. 80, p. 167
  both vowels sounded—L. 92, p. 194
eigh as long a —L. 80, p. 167
eo (both vowels sounded)—L. 92, p. 190
eo - oe—L. 92, pp. 190-191
er—L. 62, p. 130
-er not suffixed—L. 50, p. 101
er sound:
  in spelling wor, as in work—L. 63, p. 133
  spelled:
    ar, slurred as in collar—L. 62, p. 131
    ear followed by consonant, as in learn—L. 62, p. 130
    er; ir; ur; yr—L. 62, p. 130
    or, slurred as in doctor—L. 62, p. 131
    our, as in journal—L. 62, p. 130; L. 89, p. 185
-er suffix:
  meaning "more"—L. 50, p. 100
  meaning "person who or thing which does whatever root word indicates"(nouns)—L. 50, p. 101
-es suffix:
  e silent when not after hissing sound—L. 49, p. 98
  forms syllable after hissing sounds s, sh, x, z, ch—L. 49, p. 98; soft c—L. 72, p. 150; and soft g—L. 77, p. 161
-est suffix meaning "most"—L. 51, p. 103

## INDEX—(Continued)

eu (both vowels sounded)—L. 92, p. 194
eu (long u sounds)—L. 91, p. 188
ew (long u sounds)—L. 91, p. 188
ex- (prefix)—L. 53, p. 109
exceptions: (See also non-phonics.)
  angelic—L. 77, p. 161
  argue—L. 103, p. 216

  beard—L. 62, p. 131
  bull—L. 29, p. 57
  bully—L. 83, p. 172
  bush—L. 30, p. 59
  Butch—L. 31, p. 61

  cost—L. 70, p. 147

  deny—L. 83, p. 172
  doll—L. 70, p. 147

  either—L. 81, p. 169

  financier—L. 74, p. 155
  flak—L. 38, p. 72
  for—L. 16, p. 35
  frontier—L. 75, p. 157
  frost—L. 70, p. 147
  full—L. 29, p. 57

  gild—L. 69, p. 144

  height—L. 80, p. 167

  July—L. 83, p. 172

  leisure—L. 81, p. 169
  loll—L. 70, p. 147
  lost—L. 70, p. 147
  lullaby—L. 83, p. 172

  magpie—L. 45, p. 89
  moll—L. 70, p. 147

  neither—L. 81, p. 169

  occupy—L. 83, p. 172
  or—L. 16, p. 35
  orange—L. 77, p. 161

  patio—L. 75, p. 157
  pull—L. 29, p. 57
  push—L. 30, p. 59
  put—L. 29, p. 57

  sheik—L. 81, p. 169
  sleight—L. 80, p. 167
  society—L. 74, p. 155
  suite—L. 11, p. 25
  sworn—L. 63, p. 133

  too—L. 10, p. 23
  treble—L. 68, p. 142
  triple—L. 68, p. 142

  weird—L. 81, p. 169
  worn—L. 63, p. 133

  young—L. 45, p. 89
  your—L. 24, p. 48
  yours—L. 24, p. 48
  youth—L. 24, p. 48

exceptions (special categories):
  short vowel before v:
    give—L. 23, p. 46; L. 54, p. 111
    have—L. 23, p. 46; L. 54, p. 111
    love—L. 23, p. 46; L. 54, p. 111
    shove—L. 30, p. 59; L. 54, p. 111
  vowel both long and short:
    dove—L. 23, p. 46; L. 54, p. 111
    live—L. 23, p. 46; L. 54, p. 111
    wind—L. 69, p. 144
ey as long a—L. 80, p. 167
--ey as long e—L. 45, p. 89

### F

f—L. 1, p. 11
f before suffix -ed, e silent, d with sound of t—
  L. 47, p. 94
five sounds of a—L. 58, p. 119
for- (prefix)—L. 66, p. 138
fore- (prefix)—L. 66, p. 138
Foreword:
  to 1946 edition—unnumbered p. 6
  to this edition—unnumbered pp. 4-5
f sound:
  gh—L. 93, p. 197
  -lf in same syllable, 1 silent—L. 99, p. 208
  ph—L. 94, p. 198
-ften (t silent)—L. 100, p. 210
-ful (suffix)—L. 44, p. 86
--fy (verbs ending in fy; y long)—L. 83, p. 172

### G

g hard:
  L. 21, p. 43
  gh; h silent beginning or middle of word—
    L. 101, p. 212
  gu—L. 103, p. 217
  gue at end of word—L. 103, p. 216
  remains hard even when followed by e, i, or y,
    in suffixed words—L. 78, p. 164
  root words; g followed by e, i, or y—L. 78,
    p. 164
g silent:
  gm in same syllable—L. 96, p. 203
  gn in same syllable or beginning or end of
    words—L. 96, p. 202
g soft:
  as zh—L. 77, p. 162
  name sound like j—L. 77, p. 161; L. 78,
    pp. 163-164
  retaining e after soft g when next letter is not
    i or y—L. 77, p. 162
ge (soft g), same sound as j—L. 77, p. 161
ge (vowel before ge either long or short, in
  more-than-one-syllable words ending in ge)—
  L. 77, p. 162
geographical location ending (-an)—L. 74, p. 155
gg has hard sound—L. 78, p. 164

## INDEX—(Continued)

gh:
    as f—L. 93, p. 197
    gh silent:
        augh—L. 86, p. 178
        eigh (ei as long a; gh silent)—L. 80, p. 167
        igh—L. 33, p. 64
        ough—L. 87, pp. 179-180
        ough as long o, as in dough—L. 89, p. 183
        ough as ou, sound in our—L. 88, p. 181
    h silent, beginning or middle of word—L. 101, p. 212
gi (soft g), same sound as j—L. 78, p. 163
Glossary of "Sign Language"—(facing L. 1)—unnumbered p. 10
gm not in same syllable, sound both—L. 96, p. 203
gn:
    both sounded:
        generally when adding any suffix except -s, -er, -or, -ee, -ing, -ed, -ment—L. 96, p. 203
        medially in root word, but not in same syllable—L. 96, p. 203
    g silent:
        generally when adding suffixes -s, -er, -or, -ee, -ing, -ed, -ment—L. 96, p. 202
        in same syllable or at beginning or end of words—L. 96, p. 202
gu as gw—L. 103, p. 217
gu as hard g—L. 103, p. 217
gue at end of word, gue as hard g—L. 103, p. 216
gw sound (spelled gu)—L. 103, p. 217
gy (soft g), same sound as j—L. 78, p. 164

### H

h—L. 5, p. 15
h silent:
    L. 101, p. 212
    gh—L. 101, p. 212
    rh—L. 101, p. 212
hard sounds (See under c and g.)
homonyms—pp. 221-227

### I

i:
    L. 1, p. 11
    c soft when followed by i—L. 73, p. 151
    g soft when followed by i—L. 78, p. 163
    long: (See also under actual letter combinations.)
        L. 4, p. 14
        igh; i long and gh silent—L. 33, p. 64
        -ild, -ind—L. 69, p. 144
        long y changed to long i when suffix is added to verbs ending in fy and ly—L. 83, p. 172
        two consonants at beginning of word—L. 41, p. 76

i: (continued)
    short:
        L. 15, p. 32
        --ie (two-syllable words)—L. 45, p. 89
        long y changed to short i in verbs ending in fy and ly when suffix added, mainly -cation—L. 83, p. 172
        two consonants:
            at beginning of word—L. 41, p. 77
            at beginning and two at end of word—L. 41, p. 77
            at end of word—L. 27, p. 54
    y changed to i:
        in one-syllable root words; generally, when adding -ed, -er, -es, and -est—L. 82, p. 170
        when adding suffix—L. 71, p. 148; L. 82, p. 170; L. 83, p. 172
    y preceded by consonant changed to i when suffix is added—L. 82, p. 170
ia - ai—L. 92, p. 190
ia (both vowels sounded)—L. 92, p. 190
--iac; short a, but k dropped from ck digraph—L. 92, p. 193
-ic ending, in more-than-one-syllable words—L. 52, p. 106
-ick rule—L. 52, p. 106
ie as ee (long e); generally after any consonants except c and occasionally s—L. 81, pp. 168-169
ie (both vowels sounded)—L. 92, p. 194
--ie:
    adding suffix -ing—L. 46, p. 92
    as long e or short i; two-syllable words—L. 45, p. 89
    as long i—L. 4, p. 14
i_e as long i—L. 4, p. 14
igh as i (i long and gh silent)—L. 33, p. 64
-ild (words with long i, ending in two consonants without second vowel)—L. 69, p. 144
-ind (words with long i, ending in two consonants without second vowel)—L. 69, p. 144
-ing (suffix)—L. 46, p. 91
Introduction to L. 44—p. 85
io (both vowels sounded)—L. 92, pp. 191-192
io - oi—L. 92, pp. 191-192
ir—L. 62, p. 130
-ish (suffix)—L. 51, p. 103
iu (both vowels sounded)—L. 92, p. 190
iu - ui—L. 92, p. 190

### J

j—L. 20, p. 42
j sound (soft sound of g)—L. 77, p. 161; L. 78, pp. 163-164
jokes: (See also anecdotes, riddles, and stories.)
    Boys dividing a pie—L. 99, p. 209
    Girl who always came to work late—L. 83, p. 173

## INDEX—(Continued)

jokes: (continued)
   Naming wild animals (Jennie and teacher)—L. 69, p. 145

### K

k:
   L. 18, p. 38
   before -ed suffix; e silent, d with sound of t—L. 47, p. 94
   more-than-one syllable words—L. 52, p. 106
   replacement of k in ck after short vowel—L. 25, p. 50
   sound:
      c or k determined in each syllable individually—L. 52, p. 106
      ch—L. 95, p. 200
      ck—L. 19, p. 39; L. 52, pp. 106-107
      hard c—L. 19, p. 39
      -ic ending in more-than-one-syllable words—L. 52, p. 106
      -lk in same syllable—L. 99, p. 208
      qu as k—L. 103, p. 216
   spelled que at end of word—L. 103, p. 216
   "kay" sound:
      -que spelling at end of word—L. 103, p. 216
      -quet spelling at end of word—L. 103, p. 216
kn (k silent)—L. 98, p. 206
ks sound (x)—L. 35, p. 67
k-sh sound (-xi)—L. 76, p. 159
k-shun sound (-xion)—L. 76, p. 159
k-shus sound (-xious)—L. 76, p. 159
kw sound (qu)—L. 34, p. 65

### L

l:
   L. 1, p. 11
   double when adding suffix beginning with vowel, more-than-one-syllable root words ending in -ol—L. 70, p. 146
   silent:
      -ld in same syllable—L. 99, p. 208
      -lf in same syllable—L. 99, p. 208
      -lk in same syllable—L. 99, p. 208
      -lm in same syllable—L. 99, p. 208
      -lve in same syllable—L. 99, p. 208
-ld not in same syllable, sound both—L. 99, p. 208
-le:
   L. 68, p. 141
   suffixing -le words—L. 68, p. 142
   three-or-more-syllable words—L. 68, p. 142
   two-syllable words—L. 68, p. 141
-less (suffix)—L. 44, p. 86
-lf not in same syllable, sound both—L. 99, p. 208
-lk not in same syllable, sound both,—L. 99, p. 208
-lm not in same syllable, sound both—L. 99, p. 208
long a (See under a.)
long e (See under e.)
long i (See under i.)
long o (See under o.)
long oo (See under oo.)
long u (See under u.)
long vowel:
   before v—L. 23, p. 46; L. 54, p. 111
   digraph:
      backwards (both vowels sounded)—L. 92, pp. 190-191
      when not at end of root word, both vowels sounded—L. 92, p. 193
   digraphs (alphabetically indexed under actual spelling)
   diphthong, or compound combinations, both vowels sounded—L. 92, p. 194
   vowel before ge either long or short in more-than-one-syllable words—L. 77, p. 162
long y (See under y.)
-lve not in same syllable, sound both—L. 99, p. 208
-ly:
   suffix (y as i in it or long e)—Introduction to L. 44, p. 85; L. 44, p. 86
   verbs ending in ly; y long—L. 83, p. 172

### M

m—L. 1, p. 11
m sounded:
   gm in same syllable, g silent—L. 96, p. 203
   lm in same syllable, l silent—L. 99, p. 208
-mb (b silent)—L. 100, p. 210
-mb not in same syllable, sound both—L. 100, p. 210
-mn (n silent)—L. 102, p. 214
-mn not in same syllable, sound both—L. 102, p. 214
more-than-one-syllable words:
   ending in ge; vowel before ge either long or short—L. 77, p. 162
   Part II, Introduction to L. 44, p. 85

### N

n—L. 1, p. 11
n silent (mn in same syllable)—L. 102, p. 214
n sounded:
   gn, g silent, when in same syllable or beginning or ending words—L. 96, p. 202
   kn (k silent)—L. 98, p. 206
   pn (p silent)—L. 101, p. 213
-ness (suffix)—L. 44, p. 86
non-phonics: (See also exceptions.)
   ancient—L. 74, p. 155
   answer—L. 62, p. 131
   any—L. 45, p. 89
   apostrophe—L. 94, p. 198
   arc—L. 58, p. 120
   are—L. 7, p. 18; L. 57, p. 117

## INDEX—(Continued)

non-phonics: (See also exceptions.)—contd.
  baste—L. 25, p. 50
  beckon—L. 52, p. 107
  been—L. 8, p. 20
  biscuit—L. 52, p. 107
  bloc—L. 42, p. 79
  blood—L. 85, p. 176
  body—L. 45, p. 89
  both—L. 16, p. 35
  broad—L. 42, p. 79
  build—L. 27, p. 54
  built—L. 27, p. 54
  buoy—L. 90, p. 187
  busy—L. 45, p. 89
  buy—L. 12, p. 26

  carriage—L. 77, p. 163
  catacomb—L. 100, p. 210
  catastrophe—L. 94, p. 198
  choir—L. 95, p. 200
  circuit—L. 72, p. 150
  climb—L. 100, p. 210
  comb—L. 100, p. 210
  come—L. 19, p. 40
  corpuscle—L. 72, p. 150
  counterfeit—L. 88, p. 181
  coyote—L. 90, p. 187
  cyclone—L. 73, p. 152

  daily—L. 44, p. 87; L. 82, p. 171
  disc—L. 27, p. 54
  do—L. 10, p. 23
  does—L. 16, p. 35
  done—L. 16, p. 35
  don't—L. 10, p. 23
  door—L. 85, p. 176

  exaggerate—L. 78, p. 164
  eye—L. 12, p. 26
  eyes—L. 12, p. 26

  father—L. 58, p. 120
  fiery—L. 45, p. 89
  flood—L. 85, p. 176
  floor—L. 85, p. 176
  forfeit—L. 81, p. 169
  friend—L. 81, p. 169

  gauge—L. 77, p. 163; L. 86, p. 178
  gone—L. 21, p. 43
  gross—L. 42, p. 79

  haste—L. 25, p. 50
  hey—L. 9, p. 21
  hi—L. 12, p. 26
  honey—L. 45, p. 89

  jackal—L. 52, p. 107
  jeopardy—L. 92, p. 191

  kale—L. 19, p. 40
  kayak—L. 92, p. 191
  key—L. 18, p. 38
  kiln—L. 27, p. 54

non-phonics: (See also exceptions.)—contd.
  leopard—L. 92, p. 191
  lieu—L. 91, p. 188
  lieutenant—L. 91, p. 188

  many—L. 45, p. 89
  margarine—L. 77, p. 163
  marriage—L. 77, p. 163
  money—L. 45, p. 89
  mortgage—L. 77, p. 163
  much—L. 31, p. 61
  muscle—L. 72, p. 150

  niche—L. 31, p. 61
  ninth—L. 27, p. 54
  none—L. 16, p. 35

  of—L. 16, p. 35
  once—L. 72, p. 150
  one—L. 10, p. 23
  only—L. 44, p. 87

  paste—L. 25, p. 50
  people—L. 68, p. 142; L. 92, p. 191
  pint—L. 27, p. 54
  plaid—L. 38, p. 72
  poignant—L. 90, p. 187
  porpoise—L. 90, p. 187
  purpose—L. 62, p. 131

  queue—L. 34, p. 65

  receipt—L. 81, p. 169
  recipe—L. 72, p. 150
  reckon—L. 52, p. 107
  review—L. 91, p. 188
  rich—L. 31, p. 61

  said—L. 9, p. 21
  says—L. 9, p. 21
  scalp—L. 56, p. 115
  scarce—L. 72, p. 150
  sergeant—L. 77, p. 163
  sew—L. 91, p. 188
  shall—L. 56, p. 115
  shoe—L. 30, p. 59
  sieve—L. 81, p. 169
  skate—L. 37, p. 70
  skulk—L. 43, p. 81
  skull—L. 43, p. 81
  skunk—L. 43, p. 81
  soccer—L. 72, p. 150
  soldier—L. 81, p. 169
  some—L. 16, p. 35
  study—L. 45, p. 89
  such—L. 31, p. 61
  suggest—L. 78, p. 164
  sure—L. 30, p. 59
  sword—L. 63, p. 133

  talc—L. 56, p. 115
  taste—L. 25, p. 50
  their—L. 14, p. 31
  theirs—L. 14, p. 31

## INDEX—(Continued)

non-phonics: (See also exceptions.)—contd.
  there—L. 14, p. 31
  they—L. 9, p. 21
  thyme—L. 12, p. 26
  to—L. 10, p. 23
  tomb—L. 100, p. 210
  tortoise—L. 90, p. 187
  toward—L. 60, p. 123
  trek—L. 40, p. 75
  truth—L. 43, p. 81
  two—L. 65, p. 137

  valve—L. 56, p. 115
  veil—L. 23, p. 46
  vein—L. 23, p. 46
  view—L. 91, p. 188

  waste—L. 25, p. 50
  Wednesday—L. 71, p. 149
  were—L. 62, p. 131
  what—L. 32, p. 63
  where—L. 32, p. 63
  whey—L. 32, p. 63
  which—L. 32, p. 63
  who—L. 32, p. 63
  whole—L. 32, p. 63
  wholly—L. 44, p. 87
  whom—L. 32, p. 63
  whose—L. 32, p. 63
  womb—L. 100, p. 210
  women—L. 65, p. 137
  won't—L. 22, p. 45

  yak—L. 24, p. 48
  yeoman—L. 92, p. 191
  you—L. 24, p. 48

  zinc—L. 36, p. 69

noun ending -us—L. 74, p. 155

### O

--o as long o—L. 10, p. 23
o as oo long (as in do)—L. 65, p. 137
o as w—L. 103, p. 217
o like u in put—L. 65, p. 137
o like u in rude—L. 65, p. 137
o long: (See also under actual letter combinations.)
  L. 10, p. 23; L. 70, p. 146
  as in though and thorough—L. 87, p. 180
  double l when adding suffix beginning with vowel, in more-than-one-syllable root words ending in -ol—L. 70, p. 146
  -old, -olt, -ost, -oll; words with long o ending in two consonants without second vowel—L. 70, p. 146
  ou as in soul—L. 89, pp. 183-184
  ough as in dough—L. 89, p. 183
  ow as in grow—L. 89, p. 183
  two consonants at beginning of word—L. 42, p. 78
  two consonants at end of word—L. 28, p. 55

o short:
  L. 16, p. 34; L. 60, p. 123 (short o sound)
  two consonants at beginning of word—L. 42, p. 79
  two consonants at beginning and two at end of word—L. 42, p. 79
  two consonants at end of word—L. 28, p. 55
oa - ao—L. 92, p. 190
oa as long o—L. 10, p. 23
oa (both vowels sounded)—L. 92, p. 194
oar—L. 61, p. 128
oe:
  both sounded (when not at end of root word)—L. 92, p. 193
  oe - eo—L. 92, pp. 190-191
--oe as long o—L. 10, p. 23; L. 92, p. 193
o_e as long o—L. 10, p. 23
oi:
  L. 90, p. 186
  as wah—L. 103, p. 217
  both vowels sounded—L. 92, p. 194
  oi - io—L. 92, pp. 191-192
-old (words with long o, ending in two consonants without second vowel)—L. 70, p. 146
-oll (words with long o, ending in two consonants without second vowel)—L. 70, p. 146
-olt (words with long o, ending in two consonants without second vowel)—L. 70, p. 146
one-syllable words—Beginning at L. 1, p. 11
oo (both vowels sounded)—L. 92, p. 194
oo long:
  as in food—L. 84, p. 174
  spelled o, as in do—L. 65, p. 137
  spelled ou, as in soup—L. 65, p. 137; L. 89, p. 184
  spelled ough, as in through—L. 87, p. 180
oo short:
  as in book—L. 85, p. 176
  spelled ou, as in could—L. 89, p. 184
oor short; spelled our, as in tour—L. 89, p. 185
or:
  L. 61, p. 128
  slurred like er—L. 62, p. 131
  spelled our, as in four—L. 61, p. 128; L. 89, p. 185
ore—L. 61, p. 128
-ost (words with long o, ending in two consonants without second vowel)—L. 70, p. 146
ou:
  as aw (as in brought): nine sounds of ou—L. 89, p. 184
  as in out—L. 88, p. 181; L. 89 p. 183
  as long o (as in soul)—L. 89, pp. 183-184
  as long oo (as in soup)—L. 65, p. 137; L. 89, p. 184
  as short oo (as in could)—L. 89, p. 184
  as short u:
    accented, as in touch—L. 89, p. 184
    unaccented, as in delicious—L. 89, p. 185
  as u in rude—L. 65, p. 137

# INDEX—(Continued)

ou: (continued)
    nine sounds—L. 89, pp. 183-185
    ou - uo—L. 92, p. 192
oua as wa—L. 103, p. 217
ough (gh silent):
    L. 87, pp. 179-180
    as long o—L. 87, p. 180; L. 89, p. 183
    as long o or schwa sound—L. 87, p. 180
    as long oo—L. 87, p. 180
    as ou (as in bough)—L. 88, p. 181
    four words beginning with th and containing ough (different sounds)—L. 87, p. 180
our:
    as er:
        L. 62, p. 130
        as in journal—L. 89, p. 185
    as or:
        L. 61, p. 128
        as in four; nine sounds of ou—L. 89, p. 185
    as short oor (as in tour)—L. 89, p. 185
-ous ending indicates adjective—L. 74, p. 155
ow as in now—L. 88, p. 181
ow as long o (as in grow)—L. 89, p. 183
oy—L. 90, p. 187
oy - yo—L. 92, p. 192

## P

p:
    L. 8, p. 20
    before suffix -ed; e silent, d with sound of t—L. 47, p. 94
    silent:
        pn—L. 101, p. 213
        ps—L. 101, p. 213
        pt—L. 101, p. 213
Part I—One-syllable words—Starts at L. 1, p. 11
Part II—Two-syllable words, prefixes, suffixes, etc.—Starts on p. 85
Part III—Compound vowels and consonants; two vowels side by side, both sounded; two consonants side by side, one silent; homonyms—Starts at L. 84, p. 174
person ending (-an)—L. 74, p. 155
ph as f—L. 94, p. 198
pn (p silent)—L. 101, p. 213
prefix:
    a- —L. 52, p. 105
    de- —L. 53, p. 109
    ex- —L. 53, p. 109
    for- —L. 66, p. 138
    fore- —L. 66, p. 138
    per- —L. 67, p. 139
    pre- L. 67, p. 139
    pro- —L. 67, p. 139
    re- —L. 53, p. 109
    un- —L. 53, p. 109
ps (p silent)—L. 101, p. 213
pt (p silent)—L. 101, p. 213

## Q

qu as k—L. 103, p. 216
qu as kw—L. 34, p. 65
qua (sound of "a" in "all" and as short o)—L. 60, p. 123
quar (sound of "a" in "all" and as short o)—L. 60, p. 123
--que as k, at end of word—L. 103, p. 216
--que as "kay"—L. 103, p. 216
--quet as "kay"—L. 103, p. 216
Quotation, "If thou lackest knowledge"—p. 220

## R

r—L. 5, p. 15
r (spelled wr; w silent)—L. 97, p. 205
re- (prefix)—L. 53, p. 109
replacement of:
    c in ck after short vowel—L. 25, p. 50
    k in ck after short vowel—L. 25, p. 50
Review:
    compound vowels (following L. 92)—p. 196
    long vowels:
        (following L. 12), p. 28
        (following L. 60), pp. 125-127
        (following L. 92), p. 196
    ou sounds—L. 89, pp. 183-185
    short vowels:
        (following L. 43), pp. 83-84
        (following L. 60), pp. 125-127
rh (h silent)—L. 101, p. 212
riddles: (See also anecdotes, jokes, and stories.)
    Brothers and sisters—L. 50, p. 102
    Clock—L. 60, p. 124

## S

s:
    L. 5, p. 15; L. 7, p. 18; p. 228
    after s, sound ti as ch—L. 75, p. 157
    after s, suffix -es forms a syllable—L. 49, p. 98
    before suffix -ed; e silent, d with sound of t—L. 47, p. 94
    either ei or ie after s—L. 81, p. 169
    spelling ps (p silent)—L. 101, p. 213
-s (plural)—L. 7, p. 18
-s (suffix)—L. 49, p. 98
-s (third person singular)—L. 7, p. 18
's (singular possessive)—L. 7, p. 18
s' (plural possessive)—L. 7, p. 18
schwa sound:
    in arr, ara, are, ari, aro, aru, ary; before end of root word—L. 59, p. 121
    of ough (thorough)—L. 87, p. 180
scr (three consonants at beginning of word)—L. 55, p. 113
--se (at end of word)—L. 7, p. 18

# INDEX—(Continued)

seven sounds of ea—L. 64, pp. 134-135
sh:
   L. 30, p. 59
   after sh, suffix -es forms syllable—L. 49, p. 98
   before suffix -ed; e silent, d with sound of t—L. 47, p. 94
   ce as sh—L. 74, p. 155
   ci as sh: followed by vowel; not in first syllable of root word; -cial, -cian, -cient, -ciency, -ciate, -cion, -cious—L. 74, pp. 154-155
   ci as shee—L. 74, p. 154
   si as sh: after consonant and followed by vowel; not in first syllable of root word; -ssion—L. 76, p. 158
   ti as sh: followed by vowel; not in first syllable of root word; -tion, -tian, -tient, -tiate, -tial, -tious—L. 75, pp. 156-157
shal sound:
   -cial—L. 74, p. 154
   -tial—L. 75, p. 156
shan sound:
   -cian—L. 74, p. 154
   -tian—L. 75, p. 156
"she ate" sound:
   -ciate—L. 74, p. 155
   -tiate—L. 75, p. 157
shee sound (-ci)—L. 74, p. 154
shensee sound (-ciency)—L. 74, p. 154
shent sound:
   -cient—L. 74, p. 154
   -tient—L. 75, p. 157
short a (See under a.)
short e (See under e.)
short i (See under i.)
short o (See under o.)
short oo (See under oo.)
short oor (See under oor.)
short u (See under u.)
short vowel before ge (vowel either long or short); more-than-one-syllable words—L. 77, p. 162
short vowel before v—L. 23, p. 46; L. 54, p. 111
short y (See under y.)
shu sound spelled su—L. 76, p. 159
shul sound:
   -cial—L. 74, p. 154
   -tial—L. 75, p. 156
shun sound:
   -cian; -cion—L. 74, p. 154
   -sion; -sion after r—L. 76, p. 158
   -ssion—L. 76, p. 158
   -tian; -tion—L. 75, p. 156
shunsee sound (-ciency)—L. 74, p. 154
shunt sound:
   -cient—L. 74, p. 154
   -tient—L. 75, p. 157
shus sound:
   -cious—L. 74, p. 154
   -tious—L. 75, p. 156
-si as sh—L. 76, p. 158

-si as zh (after a vowel)—L. 76, p. 159
"Sign Language," Glossary of—(Facing L. 1), unnumbered p. 10
-sion as shun (after consonant)—L. 76, p. 158
-sion as zhun, shun (after r)—L. 76, p. 158
soft and hard c—L. 78, p. 164
soft c—L. 72, p. 149; L. 73, p. 151
soft g—L. 77, p. 161; L. 78, pp. 163-164
sounds of a (five)—L. 58, p. 119
sounds of consonants (chart)—p. 228
sounds of ea (seven)—L. 64, pp. 134-135
sounds of ou (nine)—L. 89, pp. 183-185
spl- (three consonants at beginning of word)—L. 55, p. 113
spr- (three consonants at beginning of word)—L. 55, p. 113
squ- (three consonants at beginning of word)—L. 55, p. 113
-ssion as shun—L. 76, p. 158
-sten (t silent)—L. 100, p. 210
-stle (t silent)—L. 100, p. 210
stories: (See also anecdotes, jokes, and riddles.)
   Ball game at beach—L. 31, pp. 61-62
   Beach outing—L. 32, pp. 63-64
   Forking of the roads (A Short, Short Story)—L. 61, p. 129
   Fox and wolf—L. 84, p. 175
   Hungry fox and chickens—L. 72, p. 150
   Man who couldn't read and little girl—L. 68, p. 142
   Men in barber shop—L. 62, p. 132
   On a Picnic—L. 52, p. 107
   Painting of portrait—L. 81, p. 169
   Praying man and king—L. 98, p. 207
   Real Charity (story of man who did good deeds)—L. 85, p. 176
   The Tongue—(following L. 103)—p. 219
str- (three consonants at beginning of word)—L. 55, p. 113
su as:
   shu (long u construction)—L. 76, p. 159
   zhu (after a vowel, long u construction)—L. 76, p. 159
suffix:
   -ed—L. 47, pp. 93-94; L. 48, p. 96
   -er—L. 50, pp. 100-101
   -es—L. 49, p. 98
   -est—L. 51, p. 103
   -ful—L. 44, p. 86
   -ing—L. 46, p. 91
   -ing added to words ending in -ie—L. 46, p. 92
   -ish—L. 51, p. 103
   -less—L. 44, p. 86
   -ly—Introduction to L. 44, p. 85; L. 44, p. 86
   -ness—L. 44, p. 86
   -s—L. 7, p. 18; L. 49, p. 98
   -y—L. 45, p. 88
suffixes (double)—L. 71, p. 148
suffixing -le words—L. 68, p. 142

# INDEX—(Continued)

summary, long vowels—Review (following L. 12)— p. 28
syllables:
  one—starting with L. 1, p. 11
  three—L. 71, p. 148
  two—starting with Introduction to L. 44, p. 85

### T

t—L. 6, p. 16
t (-bt in same syllable; b silent)—L. 100, p. 210
t (pt at beginning of word; p silent)—L. 101, p. 213
t silent:
  -ften—L. 100, p. 210
  -sten—L. 100, p. 210
  -stle—L. 100, p. 210
t sound (suffix -ed)—L. 47, p. 94
Table of Contents—unnumbered pp. 7-9
tch—L. 31, p. 61
th- (at beginning of word)—L. 7, p. 18
th (four words beginning with th and containing different sounds of ough)—L. 87, p. 180
--th (voiceless at end of word)—L. 7, p. 18
_the (long vowel before)—L. 7, p. 18
--the (voiced at end of word)—L. 7, p. 18
three consonants at beginning of word: scr-, spl-, spr-, str-, squ- —L. 55, p. 113
three consonants at end of word—L. 55, p. 114
three-syllable words—L. 71, p. 148
-ti as sh—L. 75, pp. 156-157
-ti sounded as ch after s—L. 75, p. 157
-tial as shul, shal—L. 75, p. 156
-tian as shun, shan—L. 75, p. 156
-tiate as "she ate"—L. 75, p. 157
-tient as shunt, shent—L. 75, p. 157
-tion as shun—L. 75, p. 156
-tious as shus—L. 75, p. 156
Tongue, The (story following L. 103), p. 219
tu as chu (not in first syllable of root word; long u construction)—L. 79, p. 166
two consonants side by side, one silent—L. 96, p. 202, through L. 102, p. 214
two-syllable words—Starting L. 44, p. 86
two-syllable words (and prefix a-)—L. 52, p. 105
two vowels side by side, both sounded—L. 92, pp. 190-194

### U

u—L. 11, p. 25
u as in pull—L. 54, p. 111
u as w—L. 103, p. 217
u long: (See also under actual letter combinations.)
  L. 11, p. 25
  eu—L. 91, p. 188
  ew—L. 91, p. 188
  two consonants at beginning of word—L. 43, p. 80

u short:
  L. 17, p. 36
  spelled ou:
    as in delicious, unaccented—L. 89, p. 185
    as in touch, accented—L. 89, p. 184
  two consonants:
    at beginning of word—L. 43, p. 81
    at beginning and two at end of word—L. 43, p. 81
    at end of word—L. 29, p. 57
u silent (gu spelling)—L. 103, p. 217
u sound:
  in put, spelled o as in wolf—L. 65, p. 137
  in rude, spelled:
    o as in do and lose—L. 65, p. 137
    ou as in soup—L. 65, p. 137; L. 89, p. 184
ua - au—L. 92, pp. 191-192
ua (both vowels sounded)—L. 92, pp. 191-192
ue, both sounded (when not at end of root word)—L. 92, p. 193
--ue as long u—L. 11, p. 25; L. 92, p. 193
--ue silent:
  -gue at end of word—L. 103, p. 216
  -que at end of word—L. 103, p. 216
u_e as long u—L. 11, p. 25
ui as long u—L. 11, p. 25
ui (both vowels sounded)—L. 92, p. 194
ui - iu—L. 92, p. 190
un- (prefix)—L. 53, p. 109
uo (both vowels sounded)—L. 92, p. 192
uo - ou—L. 92, p. 192
ur—L. 62, p. 130
-us ending indicates noun—L. 74, p. 155

### V

v:
  L. 23, p. 46; L. 54, p. 111
  -lve in same syllable; l silent—L. 99, p. 208
vowel:
  before:
    ge, either long or short, in more-than-one-syllable words—L. 77, p. 162
    v, both long and short—L. 23, p. 46; L. 54, p. 111
  digraph, long: (See also under actual letter combinations.)
    backwards, both vowels sounded—L. 92, pp. 190-191
    both vowels sounded—L. 92, p. 194
    when not at end of root word, both vowels sounded—L. 92, p. 193
vowels:
  a e i o u y—L. 12, p. 26
  both sounded (See vowel, digraph, long; vowels, compound; vowels, diphthongs.)
  compound:
    backwards, both vowels sounded—L. 92, pp. 191-192
    both vowels sounded—L. 92, p. 194

# INDEX—(Continued)

vowels: (continued)
  diphthongs:
    backwards, both vowels sounded—L. 92, pp. 191-192
    both vowels sounded—L. 92, p. 194
  review:
    compound vowels:
      (following L. 92), p. 196
    long vowels:
      (following L. 12), p. 28
      (following L. 60), pp. 125-127
      (following L. 92), p. 196
    short vowels:
      (following L. 43), pp. 83-84
      (following L. 60), pp. 125-127

## W

w—L. 22, p. 45; p. 228
w silent (wr)—L. 97, p. 205
w sound:
  o as w—L. 103, p. 217
  qu as kw—L. 34, p. 65
  u as w—L. 103, p. 217
wa (oua as wa)—L. 103, p. 217
wa (sound of "a" in "all" and as short o)—L. 60, p. 123
wah sound (oi as wah)—L. 103, p. 217
war (sound of "a" in "all" and as short o)—L. 60, p. 123
wer sound (spelled wor as in work)—L. 63, p. 133
wh (read hw)—L. 32, p. 63
wha (sound of "a" in "all" and as short o)—L. 60, p. 123
whar (sound of "a" in "all" and as short o)—L. 60, p. 123
wor sounded as wer—L. 63, p. 133
words of more than one syllable—Beginning with Part II, p. 85
wr (w silent)—L. 97, p. 205

## X

x—L. 35, p. 67
x (after x, suffix -es forms a syllable)—L. 49, p. 98
x as gz—p. 228
x as ks—L. 35, p. 67
x as z (beginning of word)—p. 228
x before suffix -ed; e silent, d with sound of t—L. 47, p. 94
-xi as k-sh—L. 76, p. 159
-xion as k-shun—L. 76, p. 159
-xious as k-shus—L. 76, p. 159

## Y

y:
  L. 12, p. 26; L. 24, p. 48
  as a consonant—L. 24, p. 48; p. 228

y: (continued)
  as i—L. 12, p. 26
  c soft when followed by y—L. 73, p. 151
  changed to i:
    one-syllable root words; generally, when adding -ed, -er, -es, and -est—L. 82, p. 170
    when adding a suffix—L. 71, p. 148; L. 82, pp. 170, 172
  g soft when followed by y—L. 78, p. 164
  long: (See also under actual letter combinations.)
    L. 12, p. 26; L. 83, p. 172
    two consonants at beginning of word—L. 43, p. 80
    verbs ending in fy and ly:
      L. 83, p. 172
      y changed to long i when suffix is added—L. 83, p. 172
      y changed to short i when suffix is added, mainly -cation—L. 83, p. 172
  not changed to i:
    when adding suffix beginning with i—L. 82, p. 171
    when vowel precedes y—L. 82, p. 171
  preceded by consonant, changed to i when suffix is added—L. 71, p. 148; L. 82, p. 170
  short:
    L. 15, p. 33
    two consonants at beginning and two at end of word—L. 43, p. 81
--y:
  as i—Introduction to L. 44, p. 85
  as long e (suffix -ly)—Introduction to L. 44, p. 85
  as long i—L. 12, p. 26; L. 83, p. 172
  as short i or long e sound (suffix -ly)—Introduction to L. 44, p. 85
-y, suffix, two-syllable words—L. 45, p. 88
ya - ay—L. 92, p. 191
ya (both vowels sounded)—L. 92, p. 191
ye (both vowels sounded; when not at end of root word)—L. 92, p. 193
--ye as long i—L. 12, p. 26; Introduction to L. 44, p. 85; L. 92, p. 193
y_e as long i—L. 12, p. 26
yo (both vowels sounded)—L. 92, p. 192
yo - oy—L. 92, p. 192
yr as er—L. 62, p. 130

## Z

z—L. 36, p. 69; p. 228
z (after z, suffix -es forms a syllable)—L. 49, p. 98
zh (after a vowel, sound si as zh)—L. 76, p. 159
zh (soft g spelling)—L. 77, p. 162
zhu (su sounded as zhu after a vowel; long u construction)—L. 76, p. 159
zhun sound (-sion after a vowel)—L. 76, p. 159
zhun sound (-sion after r)—L. 76, p. 158